TRAVERSE
THEATRE

Traverse Theatre Company

Green Field

by Riccardo Galgani

cast in order of appearance

Jo	Sharon Small
Robert	James Cunningham
Bill	Ewan Stewart
Viv	Molly Innes
Chris	Paul Thomas Hickey

director	Roxana Silbert
designer	Liz Cooke
lighting designer	Chahine Yavroyan
sound designed by	John Irvine
assistant director	Helen-Marie O'Malley
stage manager	Gavin Harding
deputy stage manager	Brendan Graham
assistant stage manager	Gemma Smith
wardrobe supervisor	Lynn Ferguson
wardrobe assistant	Stephanie Thorburn
scenic artist	Moley Campbell
carpenter	Hal Jones
workshop assistants	Jenny Duttine, Jamie Samuel

First performed at the Traverse Theatre
Friday 26 April 2002

TRAVERSE THEATRE
powerhouse of new writing DAILY TELEGRAPH

Artistic Director Philip Howard

The Traverse is Scotland's new writing theatre. Founded in 1963 by a group of maverick artists and enthusiasts, it began as an imaginative attempt to capture the spirit of adventure and experimentation of the Edinburgh Festival all year round. Throughout the decades, the Traverse has evolved and grown in artistic output and ambition. It has refined its mission by strengthening its commitment to producing new plays by Scottish and international playwrights and actively nurturing them throughout their careers. Traverse productions have been seen worldwide and tour regularly throughout the UK and overseas.

The Traverse has produced over 600 new plays in its lifetime and, through a spirit of innovation and risk-taking, has launched the careers of many of the country's best known writers. From, among others, Stanley Eveling in the 1960s, John Byrne in the 1970s, Liz Lochhead in the 1980s, David Greig in the 1990s to Gregory Burke in the 2000s, the Traverse is unique in Scotland in its dedication to new writing. It fulfils the crucial role of providing the infrastructure, professional support and expertise to ensure the development of a dynamic theatre culture for Scotland.

The Traverse's activities encompass every aspect of playwriting and production, providing and facilitating play reading panels, script development workshops, rehearsed readings, public playwriting workshops, writers groups, a public playwrights' platform The Monday Lizard, discussions and special events. The Traverse's work with young people is of supreme importance and takes the form of encouraging playwriting through its flagship education project, Class Act, as well as the Traverse Young Writers Group.

Edinburgh's Traverse Theatre is a mini-festival in itself THE TIMES

From its conception in the 1960s, the Traverse has remained a pivotal venue during the Edinburgh Festival. It receives enormous critical and audience acclaim for its programming, as well as regularly winning awards. The year 2001 was no different with the Traverse being awarded 2 Scotsman Fringe Firsts and two Herald Angels for its own productions *Gagarin Way* and *Wiping My Mother's Arse* and a Herald Archangel for overall artistic excellence. *Gagarin Way* also recieved a First of the Firsts award from The Scotsman.

For further information on the Traverse Theatre's activities and history, an online resource is available at www.virtualtraverse.com. To find out about ways to support the Traverse, please contact Jayne Gross, Development Manager on 0131 228 3223.

COMPANY BIOGRAPHIES

Liz Cooke (Designer) Theatre Work includes: AND ALL THE CHILDREN CRIED (West Yorkshire Playhouse; THE MAGIC TOYSHOP (Shared Experience); DESTINATION (Volcano Theatre Company); LES BLANCS (Royal Exchange, Manchester); THE HACKNEY OFFICE; THE SPIRIT OF ANNIE ROSS (Druid Theatre Company); BEHSHARAM (Soho Theatre/Birmingham Rep); SPOONFACE STEINBERG (New Ambassadors/Kennedy Centre, Washington); THE DAUGHTER-IN-LAW; THE GUESTS/GOODBYE Kiss (Orange Tree Theatre); THE BEAUTY QUEEN OF LEENANE (Sailsbury Playhouse); THE GIFT (Tricycle Theatre/Birmingham Rep); THE GLORY OF LIVING; EXPOSURE (Royal Court Upstairs); BETTER (BAC); THE COMEDY OF ERRORS (Shakespeare's Globe); COOKING WITH ELVIS (Live Theatre/Whitehall Theatre); THE IDIOT (West Yorkshire Playhouse/Tour); VOLUNTEERS (Gate).

James Cunningham (Bob): For the Traverse: ABANDOMENT. Other theatre work includes PENETRATOR (Royal Court) TRAINSPOTTING (Citizens') which were both performed at the Traverse; CLEANSED (Royal Court); MARABOU STORK NIGHTMARES (Citizens'). Television includes: MUGS GAME; PIE IN THE SKY; ROUGHNECKS 2; CASUALTY; WRITERS AND NATION. Film work includes: AMERICAN COUSINS; WAR REQUIEM; SNATCH'D; BUMPIN THE ODDS plus various short films and pop videos

Riccardo Galgani (writer) Riccardo Galgani was born in Glasgow in 1969, and grew up in Brighton and London. His first play ACTS, was produced by the Traverse in 1999 as part of the FAMILY trilogy. GREEN FIELD is his second play. Other theatre work includes: A WAY OF LIVING commissioned by the RSC. Traverse Theatre and Riccardo Galgani has the support of the Pearson Playwrights' Scheme sponsored by Pearson plc.

Paul Thomas Hickey (Chris): Trained: RSAMD. For the Traverse: OLGA; PASSING PLACES, THE ARCHITECT. Other theatre work includes: THE BACKROOM (The Bush), SAILMAKER, TWELFTH NIGHT (TAG), A.D., MACBETH, STILL LIFE, ECSTASY, WASTED (Raindog), JUMP THE LIFE TO COME (7:84 Scotland), THE SLAB BOYS TRILOGY (Young Vic), SHINING SOULS (Peter Hall Company at the Old Vic), MAINSTREAM, TIMELESS (Suspect Culture), CRAVE (Paines Plough). TV work includes: TINSEL TOWN, CARDIAC ARREST (BBC), TAGGART, HIGH ROAD, THE BRITOIL FRAUD, THE JACOBITES (STV) THE SWEETEST FEELING (Starcatch). Radio work includes several plays for BBC Radio Scotland including: BATTLE OF THE AIRWAVES, BODIES OCCUPATION, THE BASEMENT TAPES, PASSING PLACES. Film work includes: WANTING AND GETTING, THE LUCKY SUIT, CALIFORNIA SUNSHINE, LAY OF THE LAND.

Molly Innes (Viv): For the Traverse: SOLEMN MASS FOR A FULL MOON IN SUMMER; WIDOWS, SHINING SOULS, STONES AND ASHES, CROSS DRESSING IN THE DEPRESSION, DREAMING IN PUBLIC (Traverse & Byre). Other Theatre work includes: BLOODED (Boilerhouse); ANTIGONE (Tag); MOVING OBJECT (Brunton); ELECTRA (Theatre Babel); TIMELESS (Suspect Culture), DOING BIRD (Cat A Theatre Co.); PLAYBOY OF THE WESTERN WORLD (Communicado); A LISTENING HEAVEN; JECKYLL AND HYDE ,TO KILL A MOCKING BIRD, THE PRIME OF MISS JEAN BRODIE (Royal Lyceum); STINGING SEA (Citizens'); TARTUFFE (Dundee Rep); GLORIA GOODHEART AND THE GLITTER GRAB GANG, JOLLY ROBERT AND THE PIRATES FROM SPACE (Theatre Workshop); MURDER AND THE MUSIC HALL (Theatre Public). Film work includes: KARMIC MOTHERS (Tartan Short), RATCATCHER, STELLA DOES TRICKS. Television work includes: REBUS, LIFE SUPPORT, PSYCHOS, THE BILL, A MUGS GAME; TAKIN' OVER THE ASYLUM; THE FERGUSON THEORY; STRATHBLAIR; RAB C. NESBITT. Radio work includes: BILL 'N' KOO, SOME OF MY BEST FRIENDS ARE DOLPHINS, THE FOURTH FOREIGNER (BBC Radio Four).

John Irvine (composer): GREEN FIELD is John's 18th show for the Traverse. Other theatre work includes KtC, Tron Theatre, Dundee Rep, Royal Lyceum (Edinburgh), Citizens Theatre, TAG, Gate Theatre (London) and Lung Ha's. John gained his PhD in music composition in1999 from the University of Edinburgh and currently teaches at The City of Edinburgh Music School and St Mary's Music School.

Helen-Marie O'Malley (Assistant Director) Trained: RSAMD. For the Traverse: FIRST BITE 2002; COLD COME CRANES GONE. Assistant Director on: THE BALLAD OF CRAZY PAOLA; FIRST BITE 2001; HERITAGE; THE TRESTLE AT POPE LICK CREEK. Other Theatre work includes: SLEEPING AROUND (Tron); AND THEN THERE WERE NONE (Fonts). Directing and Performing: NIGHT SKY, NO MOON; NO STARS (Wisconsin, USA). Helen-Marie is a recipient of both the Bruce Millar andJohn Fernald Awards for young directors.

Roxana Silbert (Director): Currently Literary Director of the Traverse Theatre. She was previously Associate Director at the Royal Court Theatre and the West Yorkshire Playhouse and Deputy Director at Paines Plough. For the Traverse: QUARTZ. Other Theatre work includes: BRIXTON STORIES (RSC); I WAS SO LUCKY; BEEN SO LONG, FAIRGAME, BAZAAR, SWEETHEART, ESSEX GIRLS, MULES, WOUNDS TO HER FACE, VOICES FOR NINE (Royal Court); SPLASH HATCH ON THE E GOING DOWN (Donmar Warehouse), THE FAST SHOW LIVE (Phil McIntyre Productions at the Apollo Hammersmith); CHANNEL 4 SIT.COM FESTIVAL; CADILLAC RANCH (Soho Theatre); TWO HORSEMEN (Bush Theatre/ Gate Theatre – Winner of Time Out Award); THE LOVERS (Gate Theatre), PRECIOUS (West Yorkshire Playhouse); A LITTLE FANTASY (London Mime Festival with Told by an Idiot); LOVE (London Opera Festival); A SERVANT OF TWO MASKS (Sheffield Crucible); THE PRICE (Bolton Octagon); TRANSLATIONS; TOP GIRLS (New Vic). Television work includes: TABLE TWELVE (Two short Films for BBC)

Sharon Small (Jo) Previous Theatre work includes: INSIGNIFICANCE (Chitchester Festival); THE LONDON CUCKOLDS (National Theatre); THE THREEPENNY OPERA (Donmar Warehouse); ARMSTRONG'S LAST GOODNIGHT; SCHOOL FOR WIVES; TRAVESTIES (Royal Lyceum); WHAT NOW LITTLE MAN (Greenwich Studio); THE NUN (Greenwich Studio); SUDDENLY LAST SUMMER (Horseshoe Theatre); CINDERELLA (Stafford); HIMSELF (Southampton). She has also appeared in productions with Perth Theatre, Pitlochry, Colchester and various Fringe Productions. Television work includes: THE INSPECTOR LYNLEY MYSTERIES; SUNBURN; ROUGHNECKS (BBC); GLASGOW KISS (Wall to Wall); NO CHILD OF MINE (MAI); HAMISH MACBETH (Zenith); THE BILL (Thames); DR FINDLAY; TAGGART (STV); AN INDEPENDENT MAN (Witzend). Film work includes: ABOUT A BOY (Working Title); BUMPING THE ODDS (Wall to Wall); BITE (Mallinson Films); DRIVEN (Earchbound Pictures).

Ewan Stewart (*Bill*) For the Traverse: THE ORPHANS COMEDY; LUCY'S PLAY; Other Theatre work includes: AMONTH IN THE COUNTRY; DON JAUN; SERGEANT MUSGRAVE's DANCE; MAJOR BARBARA; THE MURDERERS; IN THE BLUE; AS I LAY DYING; RACING DEMON; TORQUATA TASSO; WHEN WE WERE WOMEN (National Theatre); OUR LATE NIGHT; SACRED HEART; TRADE; BLUEBIRD; THYESTES; LIVE LIKE PIGS; ROAD; FLYING BLIND.(Royal Court); SISTERS, BROTHERS (Notting Hill Gate); THE DUCHESS OF MALFI (Bristol Old Vic); A WORKING WOMAN (West Yorkshire Playhouse); PHOENIX (Bush Theatre); MIDSUMMER NIGHTS DREAM (Scottish Opera). Film work includes: CONSPIRACY; THE LAST GREAT WILDERNESS; THE CLOSER YOU GET; BIG BRASS RING; TITANIC; STELLA DOES TRICKS; ROB ROY; KAFKA; THE COOK, THE THEIF HIS WIFE AND HER LOVER; RESURRECTED; NOT QUITE IN JERUSALEM; REMEMBERANCE; WHO DARES WINS; ALL QUIET ON THE WESTERN FRONT; THAT SUMMER. Television work includes: IN DEEP; LITTLE BIRD; LOOKING AFTER JO JO; THE BILL; THE ADVOCATES; TOUCH AND GO; A MUG'S GAME; DOWN AMONG THE BIG BOYS; PARADISE POSTPONED; MACKENZIE;); THE PROFESSIONALS; RAIN ON THE ROOF; SOLIDERS TALKING (cleanly).

Chahine Yavroyan (lighting designer): Trained at the Bristol Old Vic Theatre School. For the Traverse: GAGARIN WAY; WIPING MY MOTHER'S ARSE; KING OF THE FIELDS, THE SPECULATOR, DANNY 306 + ME (4 EVER), PERFECT DAYS, KILL THE OLD TORTURE THEIR YOUNG, ANNA WEISS, KNIVES IN HENS, THE ARCHITECT AND SHINING SOULS. He has worked extensively in theatre, with companies and artists including: Crucible, Royal Court, Nottingham Playhouse, Leicester Haymarket, ICA, ENO, Lindsay Kemp, Rose English, Pip Simmons. Dance work includes: Yolande Snaith Theatredance, Bock & Vincenzi, Anatomy Performance Company, Naheed Saddiqui. Chahine has also worked on many site specific works including Station House Opera, Dreamwork at St Pancras Chambers, Coin St Museum, City of Bologna, Italy New Year's Eve celebrations. Fashion shows for Givenchy, Chalayan, Clemens-Riberio, Ghost. He is also a long standing People Show Person.

SPONSORSHIP

Sponsorship income enables the Traverse to commission and produce new plays and to offer audiences a diverse and exciting programme of events throughout the year.

We would like to thank the following companies for their support:

CORPORATE ASSOCIATE SCHEME

Sunday Herald
Scottish Life the PENSION company
United Distillers & Vintners
Laurence Smith & Son Wine Merchants
Willis Corroon Scotland Ltd
Wired Nomad
Alistir Tait FGA - Antiques & Fine Jewellery
Nicholas Groves Raines - Architects
KPMG
Amanda Howard Associates
Alan Thienot Champagne

Bairds Fine and Country Wines
Communicate
The Wellcome Trust

MAJOR SPONSORS

The Traverse Trivia Quiz in association with Tennants

with thanks to: Navy Blue Design Consultants & Stewarts, graphic designers and printers for the Traverse
Arts & Business for management and mentoring services
Purchase of the Traverse Box Office, computer network and technical and training equipmen has been made possible with money from The Scottish Arts Council National Lottery Fund

The Traverse receives financial assistance for its educational and development work from Calouste Gulbenkian Foundation, John Lewis Partnership, Peggy Ramsay Foundation, The Yapp Charitable Trusts, Binks Trust, The Bulldog Prinsep Theatrical Trust, Esmee Fairbairn Trus Gannochy Trust, Gordon Fraser Charitable Trust, The Garfield Weston Foundation, JSP Pollitzer Charitable Trust, The Hope Trust, The Steel Trust, Paul Hamlyn Foundation, The Craignish Trust, Lindsay's Charitable Trust, Tay Charitable Trust, Ernest Cook Trust, The Education Institute of Scotland, supporting arts projects produced by and for children.

Charity No. SC002368

For generous help on GREEN FIELD, the Traverse thanks:

LEVER BROTHERS for wardrobe care

habitat

Frasers, Edinburgh

and everyone who kindly assisted in
the making of this production.

Sets, props and costumes for GREEN FIELD created by Traverse Workshops
(funded by the National Lottery)

 Scottish
Arts Council

production photography Kevin Low
Print Photography Euan Myles

TRAVERSE THEATRE - THE COMPANY

GREEN FIELD

Riccardo Galgani

in memory of
Mary and Michael McElhone

Characters

JO, *thirty-six*

BILL, *forty-three*

ROBERT (BOB), *twenty-five*

VIV, *thirty-six*

CHRIS, *thirty-seven*

(KATIE), *thirty-seven*

The play takes place outside Glasgow, in the present day.
Setting: a new house on a green field site.

ACT ONE

The three rooms seen in the house are all immaculate. They resemble exactly the unlived-in rooms of a 'show house', with very few personal objects, only a few 'well chosen', decorative ones. Nothing is out of place, nothing is old, there is nothing with a history or a past, everything is new, derivative, designed and mass-produced. The characters, too, are all well-dressed in quality, high-street designer clothes. They are not brash or gaudy but co-ordinated and tasteful. BOB, however, although not scruffy, has not 'thought' too much about what he is wearing. He has, all the same, made some effort.

Here in the living room two new pale yellow sofas face each other. A cabinet stage right. An armchair behind it. A few books (for decoration) on lamp tables, pot pourri, candles, cushions, draped curtains, old Italianate architecture prints of columns, doorways, window frames. The walls are yellow, blue, green, variously with wallpaper, paint and borders. Door to the kitchen, front stage right, and to the unseen hallway and front door, rear stage left.

JO, wearing a simple black dress, comes into the room from the kitchen with a plate of 'nibbles'. She puts them on the cabinet and a window at the rear. She then inspects the room. She straightens the photograph on the cabinet. On the window sill she centres the vase and straightens the curtains. She steps back and looks at the windows. The chair in the back right hand corner catches her eye. She looks at it, it seems out of line and she says 'That's not right'. She goes to straighten it. As soon as her hands touch the chair the doorbell rings. She leaves immediately. BOB, good looking, then comes into the room. He carries a bottle of wine. He puts the bottle of wine by the photograph on the cabinet. He sees the nibbles and, with his jacket still on, takes one and sits down. He looks in the direction of the TV (which is off). JO comes into the doorway, holding a bunch of daffodils, and then turns.

JO (*calling upstairs*). Katie. Use the one in our room, okay. And maybe sit down for a minute and have a glass of water. I'm sure it'll pass. (*She looks in at* BOB *and as though procrastinating calls again*.) I'll see to everything down here, make sure Robert's comfortable, okay. And put these in water. Thank you again. They're beautiful. Oh, and you can just leave your coat on the bed.

JO *remains at the door for a moment, then comes into the room, closing the door behind her. She looks at* BOB *who continues, as before, looking at the television, the only variation being that he is now chewing.*

JO. So, Robert.

BOB. Bob.

JO. Bob. Sorry. Bob. (*Beat.*) I can't tell you how nice it is to have you round for dinner at last.

BOB. Is that right?

JO. Oh yes. Katie's told us so much about you. She's forever on the phone to me or Bill with some piece of news or other!

BOB. O aye?

JO. I haven't seen her this excited in ages. And now I have a face to put to the name. Bob. And we can get to know you properly ourselves. Yes. (*Pause.*) So. Bob. What about yourself?

BOB. What about myself?

JO. What is it you do?

BOB. I work for the removals.

JO. Is that right?

BOB. I drive a van.

JO. And have you been doing it for long?

BOB. In wi the bricks.

JO. You must like it then.

BOB. What's there to like?

JO. Oh it must be lovely being out and about all day.

BOB. I'm sitting in a van is what I am.

JO. But you must see some of the country at least.

BOB (*matter of fact*). The country!? I tell you, the road
ahead's about all I see.

Silence. She looks at the flowers.

JO. But it's been good to you in other ways.

BOB. How's that?

JO. Meeting Katie.

BOB. O aye.

JO. She said you helped her move.

BOB. I shifted a few boxes anyway.

JO. She's always been one for moving.

BOB. The other lads do most of the lifting.

JO. But you must've made an impression.

BOB. Aye well, I was the one she sat up in the cabin with.

Silence.

JO. Well, let's hope she settles where she is now.

BOB. She won't be there long.

JO. Don't you think?

BOB. A wee poky place like that.

JO. Is it small?

BOB. Aye, a wee poky place I said.

*Silence. JO looks at the floor, sees a few crumbs on the
carpet and picks them up.*

JO. Yes. So you did. A wee poky place. Well. I'm sure it suits
her needs. (*Seeing nibbles.*) Nibbles. (*Getting up.*) Would
you like a nibble Bob?

BOB. I'd love one.

JO. Hiding them away over here.

BOB. O aye.

JO. There you go.

BOB. Fantastic.

JO. As an appetiser. (*Puts plate down and lifts the wine bottle.*) And is this your wine?

BOB. Katie got it.

JO. That's good of her. I'll put it out of the way.

BOB. Wee fish ones these are.

JO. Prawns.

BOB. They're great.

JO. They're easy enough to make yourself. Believe you me, it doesn't take a lot of brains to make prawn nibbles! (*Putting wine on cabinet.*) I miss using my brain. It doesn't take many brains to hoover and clean and cook! (*Beat.*) I used to be a nurse. Me and Katie trained together. Did she mention that? That we were at nursing school together.

BOB (*continuing to eat*). She didn't, no.

JO. Not a word?

BOB. Not that I remember.

JO. That's where we met. We were students and then worked together at the Rob Royston Hospital. Not that it's there anymore. New houses now I think. Originally I was going to go abroad and work but I met Bill, he was the older man, and so on and so forth. I won't bore you with the details! (*Beat.*) And now it's all change in Katie's life as well.

BOB. Is that right?

JO. Well, new flat, new man . . .

BOB. Oh aye.

JO. New job. Hopefully. Do you know she laughed at me for leaving work to start a family and now she's leaving. I half thought, with the age she is, she might be thinking of starting a family herself. The two of you.

BOB. A family!?

JO. She's always wanted one.

BOB (*choking*). Christ.

JO. From the way she talks about you.

BOB. I'm not thinking of starting anything.

JO. I was just wondering.

BOB. We've only . . .

Interrupted by the sound of the front door closing followed by:

BILL (*off-stage*). Hello there.

JO. That's Bill.

BILL (*off-stage*). It's only me.

JO. My husband. You and Bill will have plenty to talk about at any rate.

BILL. What's that?

BILL, wearing a suit and coat, enters holding a newspaper. For a moment he seems nervous but very quickly composes himself.

JO. I'm just saying you and Robert/

BOB. Bob.

JO. Bob. You and Bob will have plenty to talk about.

BILL. I wasnae goin' to ignore him all night. Bob.

BILL offers his hand and puts the paper down on the table.

BILL. I'm Bill.

BOB. Bill. (*Getting up.*) Bob.

BILL. Stay where you are. (BOB *sits.*) Nice to meet you.

BOB. You too.

BILL (*to* JO). Hello love.

JO. Hello.

BILL. How . . .

    BILL *awkwardly kisses her cheek.*

JO. Oh!

BILL. There. How's yourself?

JO. Me?

BILL. Aye, you. Who else?

JO. I'm okay.

BILL. Good. And looking very well.

JO. I am?

BILL. Oh aye. Lovely.

JO. Thank you.

BILL. Lovely dress.

JO. Thank you very much.

BILL. Aye.

JO. It's something I've been saving.

BILL. Worth the wait. Aye. And everything's under control in the kitchen? Dinner in the oven? Table's set?

JO (*lifted*). Yes, yes.

BILL. Smashing.

JO (*excited*). Everything's fine. I have to confess I was a bit worried earlier, only a little bit! I've been having a frantic time all day Bob, trying to get everything ready. But no, not now, no, now I'm absolutely fine. I think I can let myself relax a little.

BILL. You do that.

JO. Having everyone together. Oh! I just can't wait for all of us to sit down and have a meal. It'll be lovely. It's been so long . . . And having you . . .

BILL. What?

JO. Seeing you/

BILL. You see me every day.

JO. I know I do. But seeing you . . . (*Quietly.*) Happy.

BILL (*loudly*). Happy? Cripes. I'm always happy. What are you talking about? What's not to be happy about, eh son?

BOB. I don't know.

BILL. Nothing.

BOB. Aye.

BILL. Nothing at all. (*Sits.*) Aye. Well. Happy. Aye. (*Beat.*) So, you're Bob then.

BOB. I am.

BILL. Katie tells me you're in removals.

JO. I forgot!

BOB. I drive a van for them anyway.

BILL. That's a place to start.

BOB. O aye.

BILL. Our paths might well have crossed you know.

BOB. How's that?

BILL. Probably crossed without us even knowing.

BOB. Can't say I've ever seen you.

BILL. I'm in storage.

JO. That's what I was going to say.

BOB. Who's that for then?

JO. When you came in.

BILL. McCullocks.

BOB (*leaning forward in his chair*). McCullocks? O aye, I know McCullocks well. I've made plenty of drops at McCullocks. You work for them then?

BILL. Bill McCullocks.

BOB. Bill?

BILL. Aye.

BOB. Is that you?

BILL. The very same.

JO. You see.

BOB. Down by the docks?

BILL. That's the one.

BOB. That old factory.

JO. He built the business up himself.

BILL. I started with a shed in Paisley. In 1989.

JO. He was very ambitious. (*Proudly.*) Absolutely bursting over with energy and enthusiasm.

BILL. I expanded that shed and bought an old warehouse in Motherwell. I've eight sites now. One in the East End. One in the town centre. Cumbernauld, the Mearns. That factory. Which I converted myself. And Rutherglen.

BOB (*sitting back in his chair*). Eight?

BILL. Aye. The second biggest storage facility in the West of Scotland.

BOB. You must do well out of a business like that.

BILL. I do alright.

JO. You two could join forces.

BOB. I only drive a van.

JO. I know but/

BILL. But what? He moves, I store?

JO. You'd be set for life.

BILL. Millionaires.

BOB (*with the extreme indifference of impossibility*). O aye, millionaires. (*Beat.*) Is that the *Evening Times* there?

BILL. Help yourself.

BOB. Ta.

BOB *picks up the paper and starts reading. Pause.* BILL *takes one of the nibbles,* JO *hands him a napkin.*

BILL. So where's Katie then Jo?

JO. She's gone to the ladies.

BILL. She's taking her time.

JO. She wasn't feeling very well.

BILL. What's wrong with her?

JO. I don't know.

BILL. How did she look when she arrived?

JO. She looked fine when she arrived. How do you expect her to look?

BILL. I don't expect her to look like anything.

Pause.

JO. What did you do with the wine?

BILL. What wine?

JO. The wine you were supposed to get.

BILL. Katie said she'd bring a bottle.

JO. When did she tell you that?

BILL. When I spoke to her on the phone.

JO. When did she phone you?

BILL. What?

JO. Nothing. (*Beat.*) One bottle won't be enough for an evening anyway.

BILL. I suppose not.

JO. You'll have to go back out.

BILL. I'm just in the door.

BOB. I saw a Tesco's down the road.

BILL. I know there's a Tesco's down the road.

BOB. Great big place.

BILL (*standing*). It's a massive development. Massive. Like everything else out here. Unbelievable.

BOB. Is that right?

BILL. It is, aye. These Green Field sites are going up everywhere. Soon they'll be all over the place. And not just in this country either, in America and Australia, and probably Russia now as well. In fifty years' time all the town centres will be empty. Everyone with any sense or money is moving out to these. The man over the road there's an area manager for Pizza Hut. Next door's an accountant. His wife does something as well, human resources or something. A new school's just opened this year and there's a hospital planned as well.

JO. So they keep saying anyway. I was actually hoping to work there.

BILL. I'm sure it'll be finished by then.

BOB. I didn't see any o' that.

BILL. Everything's still in progress. You have to remember there was nothing here before.

JO. It was farmland and fields.

BILL. They grew no crops here for years.

JO. It was very striking countryside though.

BILL. A lot of mud.

JO. We came out here once or twice when we were children for walks and remember Bill we drove out here years ago and didn't we have a picnic or something by the little lake, near that old farm cottage?

BILL. Lake! A pissy pond more like, more of a puddle than a pond even, which they've since filled I hasten to add. The place was ripe for development, ripe, and when they showed us the plans and what they were going to do it looked fantastic, didn't it Jo?

JO. In a way.

BILL. Come on, you have to admit it was ideal. The parks and the gardens.

JO. I liked the hedgerows and miniature bushes on the model!

BILL. That's a woman's mentality. Small. No vision. Each
street Bob was laid out with detached, semi-detached
houses – this is a detached by the way – with names like
The Grosvenor or The Derby. All with garages – we've got
a double – and driveways of their own, every single detail
was thought out. And as soon as they'd finished one or two
of the houses we came straight out here to see the show
house and I thought it was spectacular.

JO. We fell in love with it.

BILL. We!? I feel in love with it Jo. Not you. Don't start
pretending things now. She, if you remember sweetheart,
took a bit of persuading. She wanted somewhere in town.
One o' they old houses up the West End.

JO. But we soon agreed.

BILL. We did, aye. Eventually.

JO. Bill said that only when we moved here would our lives
begin properly, that only a complete new start would do. He
was so exuberant, it was infectious. He's a great salesman.

BILL. It's not sales, it's common sense. I've earned my money.
I'm not going to pay over a quarter of a million pounds for
a draught in the West End. A draught that someone else has
lived in. (*Beat.*) We saw the show house and bought it
outright there and then. There was no question.

BOB. This is the show house?

JO. The very same.

BILL. We could've moved in that day and never missed a thing
from the old place. Isn't that right Jo?

JO. I suppose so, almost, anyway.

BILL. Almost! (*To* BOB.) Can they ever just agree with you?
(*Beat.*) But as it was we were still the first ones out here.
It was a bit more pricey than the other ones but it came
with everything. PVCu Double Glazed windows, fenced
rear garden, turfed front garden, outside tap, Brass Lever

furniture. Even the towel radiator in the fourth bedroom's en suite was there.

BOB. Some house.

BILL. And the shaver point. (*Beat.*) It's not bad.

BOB. A good size.

BILL. It's big enough.

BOB. And it's just the two of yous?

BILL. Aye.

JO. But we had . . .

BILL. Jo.

JO. Sorry.

BILL. Aye.

JO. Yes.

BILL. Just the two of us Bob.

Silence.

JO. But we'll have a full house tonight anyway! I've set the table up in the dining room, Bill, can you even remember the last time we ate in there.

BILL. I can't, no.

JO. It's such a shame not to use it more often. And Chris and Viv Donaldson are coming over as well.

BILL. What!?

JO. Chris and Viv are coming over.

BILL. Tonight?

JO. Yes tonight.

BILL. You didn't tell me anything about Chris and Viv.

JO. I tried to phone.

BILL. Coming here?

JO (*pointed*). I couldn't get through.

BILL. I thought they were in Florida for three weeks.

JO. Two weeks Bill.

BILL. Christ almighty.

JO. They're lovely people.

BILL. Viv and Chris!?

JO. We're all very close. Me and Viv were at school together Bob. And now with Katie, well, we're practically sisters!

BILL. Did they invite themselves over? I bet they fucking did as well. Anything for a free feed.

JO. Has Katie ever mentioned them to you.

BILL. I don't believe it.

JO. Bob?

BOB. What's that?

JO. Has Katie ever mentioned Chris and Viv Donaldson to you?

BOB (*continuing to read*). She's said nothing to me about no one.

JO. You'll like them. They're just back from their holiday.

BOB. Is that right?

BILL (*gets up and with anger*). Aye, two weeks in Florida.

Pause.

JO. Bill and I were originally going to go with them.

BILL (*pacing*). O aye. Don't start on that one.

JO. I'm not starting/

BILL (*agitated*). Then you'll really get me going.

JO. We didn't go because Bill/

BILL (*anger and irritation growing*). It wasnae 'cos of me we didnae go.

JO. No, I know.

BILL. What a palaver that episode was.

JO. If you'll let me finish.

BILL. Excuse me Ginger. Take the floor.

Pause.

JO. Thank you. (*Aside.*) There's no need to be like that. (*Beat.*) Bill liked the idea of going to Florida Bob but I wanted to go to Italy or somewhere like that, somewhere with a bit of history.

BILL. What's Florida got if it hasn't got history?

JO. You know what I mean.

BILL. What do you call the space centre?

JO. I don't mean it doesn't have any history.

BILL (*abrupt*). What do you mean then?

JO. I mean somewhere European. European history. (*To* BOB.) I love travelling to places like Rome or Athens or Madrid. If I could it would be my dream to go permanently from place to place, never stopping, without ever unpacking. From St. Stephen's to St. Mark's to St. Salvador's. They're immaculate those places and it's amazing to think Bob that people built them without any of the machinery or technology that we have today and they're still standing. But they had faith and believed in God and I suppose that/

BILL. See the crap you come out with Jo.

JO. Bill . . . what . . .

BILL. Bob, I'm standing here . . . 'God?' . . . you don't want to listen to her, listen to me, I'll tell you something about travelling. I can't get Jo there out of that front door to go half a mile down the road to Tescos never mind the travel agents. Rome!? The only travelling she does is from the living room to the bathroom to the kitchen to the bedroom and the only old buildings she sees are the ones hanging on these four fucking walls.

JO. That's not true.

BILL. Not true!

JO. Not true at all.

BILL. She hasn't even stepped out into the garden for nearly three years.

JO. Bill . . . please . . . I'm sorry Bob.

BILL. You don't have to fucking apologise to him.

JO. Has Katie told you she and I went to Venice together?

BILL. Venice!?

JO. We went to Venice when . . .

BILL. Now we're talking history. Ancient fucking history.

BILL's phone rings and he answers it promptly. JO *does not react to this as it 'happens all the time'.*

BILL (*on the phone*). Hello . . . Aye . . .

JO. It wasn't that long ago.

BILL. . . . uhuh . . . uhuh . . . WHAT? . . . not . . . wait a minute . . .

BILL leaves the room.

JO. We went together before I was married. Me and Katie. I was nineteen. It was the first time I'd been abroad and I didn't even know places like that existed. I was on the verge of tears half the time it was so beautiful. When you heard the voices on the radio and saw the people on the balconies you knew you were in another world entirely. It's hard to believe I was there! Look. Wait a minute. These are from there. These glasses. (JO *goes to the cabinet and removes a Venetian glass. She handles it with tremendous care and returns to* BOB.) See . . . I was there. I need to remind myself sometimes! Each one's hand made, each one's individual – we saw them being blown in the factory. We took a Vaporetto across the Laguna Viva to Murano. That's an island, where they make all the glass. It's known as the island of glass, did you know that?

BOB. No, I didn't.

JO. A lovely name.

BOB. I've never been to Venice.

JO. You have to go. You have to make a point of going. (*Pause.*) The island of glass. (*Pause.*) Full of Italian craftsmen. They've been making the glass there for over seven hundred years. See there. That one's got a mark there and that one hasn't. And this one has a touch there. You can tell time's been spent on them, that hands have made them and even if you were to study them for hours you'd always notice something different. (*She looks quietly at the glass for a few moments.*) But anyway, that was Venice and a long time ago. (*Beat.*) We're lucky to live so close to Glasgow.

BOB. O aye, blessed.

JO. It's a lovely city as well. You must tell me, I heard they've just about finished all the work on Buchanan Street, I'm dying to see it, what's it like?

BILL *comes back into the room.*

BILL. Alright . . . Bye for now.

BILL *comes off the phone.*

JO. I was just telling Bob about Venice.

BILL. That's a great story that one.

JO. It's put me in the mood for some music.

JO *puts on a CD, Vivaldi, Autumn, Allegro (*La Caccia*) and BILL goes for his coat. As soon as it starts . . .*

BILL. Don't make the lad listen to this.

JO. It's Vivaldi.

BILL. For the umpteenth time.

JO (*to BOB*). He was Venetian as well you know.

BILL. Aye, and so are the blinds upstairs.

JO (*firmly*). Ssshhh.

BILL. Why don't you show him them.

JO *goes to BILL and touches his arm very tenderly. He recoils.*

JO (*gently*). It's something I like.

BILL. Bob's not impressed.

JO (*laughing it off*). I'm not trying to impress anyone. (*Puts off the CD.*) You have to ruin it.

She starts to leave the room.

BILL. Where are you going?

JO. To check on Katie.

BILL. I'm just away to get the wine.

JO. I'll only be a minute.

BILL. The man's sitting there without a drink.

BOB. Don't go to any bother over me.

BILL. It's no bother Bob.

BOB. No, really.

JO. There's a bottle over there anyway.

BOB. A beer's fine for me.

JO. You can drink that.

BOB. I'd love a beer.

JO leaves.

BILL. For fuck's sake. What's she like, eh? Christ, can't leave a woman alone for a minute. If that's what she wants. (*Directing his voice upstairs.*) If she wants a minute to herself.

BILL looks at BOB who is perfectly detached. BILL looks at the bottle and then picks it up, removing the tissue paper.

BILL. Let me get you a drink then.

BOB. Katie bought that.

BILL. Is that right?

BOB. Aye.

BILL. It'll be a nice wine then.

BOB (*getting up*). She got it for dinner.

BILL. She knows a thing or two about wines. Me. I'm piss
ignorant. (*Showing* BOB *the bottle*.) This'll be a good one.

BOB. It's for when we're eating.

BILL. I'm sure she'll no mind if we have a bit now. It's
something I wouldn't mind knowing about. Wine. I got a
book once but didn't get past the first page. Everything
I know I picked up in the supermarket. I know that place
like the back of my hand. Very informative – where's she
put the corkscrew? – all arranged by country. Chile. South
Africa. Bulgaria.

BOB (*looking closely at the photo on the cabinet*). Isn't that
Govan there?

BILL. What?

BOB. Govan, there. In that photo.

BILL. Oh aye.

BOB. Is that where you're from then?

BILL. It's my old place anyway. A long time ago that was
now. It's got nothing to do with me anymore. That's me an'
Jo when we were first married. (*Pause*.) That was our first
house together.

BOB. That's a flat.

BILL. Aye, I know it's a flat. It's a flat in a house. I couldn't
wait to get out of that stinking place. It disgusted me. The
reek of it.

BOB. Ma Nan lived round there.

BILL. You'll know what I'm talking about then.

BOB. I know exactly what you're saying pal.

BILL. Aye. Right. Jo would've been happy staying there but
I wish I'd never seen the place. I wish I'd never been near
it. The sight of it. What's Jo got that out for. I don't need
all these reminders. (*Putting photo away.*) I need that . . .

JO (*off-stage*). Bill.

BILL (*to* BOB). Just keep quiet. (*Beat.*) If you ignore her she sometimes goes away.

Silence.

JO (*off-stage*). Bill.

BILL. Fuck. Aye.

JO (*off-stage*). Can you come here?

BILL. What for?

JO (*off-stage*). Can I have a word please.

BILL. I'm talking.

JO (*off-stage*). Will you just come here a minute.

BILL. For crying . . . Bob, help yourself. (*He passes* BOB *the bottle of wine.*) The glasses are in there. Don't bother pouring one for Jo. She doesn't drink.

JO (*off-stage*). Bill, can you come here now?

BILL. She just drives others to it.

BILL *leaves the room.* BOB *gets two of the very elaborate, Venetian glasses out of the cabinet. Loud noise upstairs of a door slamming. He knocks the glass against the cabinet and it breaks on the floor.*

BOB. Fuck.

He picks up the pieces. He hears the sound of BILL *and/or* JO *return. He puts the pieces of glass behind the armchair in the far corner of the room and returns to the cabinet. The sound of* JO *saying 'Just have a look, will you?' is heard from the unseen hallway before* JO *enters and the front door closes. She looks at* BOB *briefly and at the wine glass. She is hurried as she seems to be simply passing through the living room on the way to the kitchen.*

Your man said to open the bottle.

JO. You don't have to do that.

JO *goes to the cabinet and, without looking in the cupboard, puts the Venetian glass back in and removes the corkscrew.*

Just sit down. I'll get you a drink in a minute. And some food. You must be hungry.

BOB. I could eat something.

JO. Well I've made a roast.

BOB. A piece and chips is what I've had the day.

JO. And for afters I've made a cheesecake.

BOB. I love cheesecake.

JO. With fresh strawberries?

BOB. O aye, I'm mad for that cheesecake.

JO. I'll get you some more nibbles for the moment.

BOB. Smashing. Some more of they wee fish ones.

JO *takes the plate from the coffee table and goes into the kitchen.* BILL *returns and goes straight to the cabinet.*

BILL. You found the corkscrew.

BOB. No bother.

BILL. Crack it open. (*He takes out two Venetian glasses, pulling at door as he does so.*) Useless thing. It's only two years old as well. There's nothing in this house more than three years old. Doesn't fucking open though. Swedish. Put them together myself in half an hour. I've a good mind to put an ad in the paper and get shot of it. I'll get a hundred, hundred and fifty for it. If you give me a hundred and twenty you can walk away with it the night.

BOB. Me?

BILL. Aye.

BOB. Now?

BILL. Cash sale. Done deal.

BOB. I've got a wee unit.

BILL. You can always use another. Sturdy. (*He tests it, it seems fragile.*) Built to last.

JO *returns, without a plate of nibbles.*

JO (*to* BILL). You weren't very long.

BILL. I was as long as it took to look.

> BILL *is about to pour the wine into one of the glasses.*

JO. What are you doing with them?

BILL. What?

JO. You can't use them.

BILL. Why not?

JO. They're my good ones.

BILL. Get away with you, good ones.

JO. I'm saving them.

BILL. For what?

JO. A special occasion.

BILL (*utterly dismissive*). What special occasion's that then?

JO. I don't know.

BILL. Well how about the night? Let's say tonight's a special occasion because, by the way it's shaping up, you know, it's fucking well looking like one.

JO. That's not funny.

BILL (*pours a little*). Have a drink out of your precious glasses.

JO (*taking the bottle*). Will you forget about that for a minute.

BILL. This'll be a first.

JO (*taking glass*). Ask Bob Bill.

BILL. Oi.

JO. Ask him.

BILL. Bob.

BOB. What's that?

BILL. Well . . . aye . . . it's nothing really.

JO. It's not nothing.

BILL. Do you know where Katie might be?

BOB. It's your house man.

BILL. Aye, I know whose house it is.

JO. She's not in the house.

BILL. No.

JO. This is the problem.

BILL. Aye.

JO. She's disappeared.

BILL. Seemingly.

JO. We've looked all over.

BILL. Upstairs and downstairs.

JO. She's not in the gardens either?

BILL. No.

JO. Front or back.

Blackout.

ACT TWO

*Dining room. A table is set for dinner in the centre of the
stage, six places. Place cards in soup bowls. A glass top table,
napkins with napkin rings, candles, various arrangements
of gold-painted pine cones and apples in glass bowls. To the
back large patio doors which, for the moment, are blackened
outside. More Italianate paintings, this time of vases and urns.
The room is decorated in burgundy and gold. A Venetian glass
is on the table with a drop of red wine in the bottom.*

BILL *has his coat on and seems to be lingering.* JO *and* BOB
sit at the table.

JO (*to* BILL). Do you think Bob would like a bowl of soup
while we're waiting.

BILL. How would I know what he'd like.

JO. Bob, would you like a bowl of soup while we're waiting?

BOB. I'd love a bowl.

JO. Will you take a roll and butter with that?

BILL. Of course he'll take a roll and butter.

JO. I was asking him.

BOB. Aye, I'll have a roll and butter.

JO. Crusty or soft?

BOB. Soft.

BILL. Who doesnae take a roll and butter?

JO. I'm just trying to keep busy.

JO *exits right.*

BILL. What are they like?

BOB. Tell me about it.

BILL. Soup!

BOB. I know.

BILL. At a time like this. Thinking about soup. Well. (*Beat.*) She makes a nice soup anyway. It's got a nice sweet taste to it. Something to do with the carrots.

JO returns with two rolls on a plate. Puts them on the table. Sits. Silence.

JO. I hope she's alright.

BILL. She'll be taking some air.

JO. You looked in the gardens.

BILL. She'll be out for a walk then.

JO. Where would she go for a walk?

BILL. Where anyone else would go.

JO. There's nowhere to walk.

BILL. Aye there is.

JO. No there's not. There's nowhere to walk and there's nothing to walk on.

BILL. There's wee paths by the roads.

JO. You know you can't walk on them.

Silence.

BOB. It's some night as well.

BILL. Don't you start.

BOB. It's muck out there.

BILL. A bit of rain.

BOB. I wouldnae want to be out the night.

BILL. She doesnae need any encouragement pal.

BOB. And they roads.

JO. See.

BILL. See what.

BOB. They're not fully made.

BILL. Get away.

BOB. They're diabolical man.

BILL. There's nothing wrong with them.

BOB. Yi cannae see a thing either.

BILL. There's lights.

BOB. T' fuck. The place is a building site.

BILL. Well, not everything's finished.

BOB. Not everything? (*Beat.*) Not anything.

Pause.

JO. That's what I've been telling you. That's what I've been trying to tell you for absolutely ages. The roads have been like that since we moved here. There's no signs or crossings and the cars drive so fast. It's not safe here Bill. You know that. You know that as well as me.

BILL. See what you've started now pal.

JO. And you said you'd go out and look for her.

BILL. Alright. Give us a minute. Okay. It's pissing down.

Pause.

JO. I thought maybe you'd like a baked potato as well?

BILL (*disbelief*). A potato?

JO. Aye, a potato.

BILL. What would he want a potato for?

JO. He's only had a chip sandwich all day. Bob?

BOB. If it's no bother.

BILL. I thought you'd cooked dinner?

JO. I've spent all day cooking dinner.

BILL. Soup and potatoes?

JO. No, not soup and potatoes. I had them done anyway.

BILL. Is that all you do all day?

JO. Are you still here?

BILL. Not for much longer.

JO. Good.

BILL. Aye.

JO. Okay.

BILL. Right. I'm away. I'm away to t' find Katie. (*Beat.*) I'll see you later then.

> BILL *heads for the door.*

BOB. And pal.

BILL. What?

BOB (*putting his hand in his pocket*). Gonnae go and get us a few beers when you're out?

BILL. Beer?

BOB. Aye.

BILL. Whatever you want.

BOB. A few tins.

BILL. Keep your money.

BOB. No offence boss.

> BOB *puts his money back in his trouser pocket.* BILL *tries to leave.* JO *follows.*

JO. And make sure you have a good look.

BILL. What are you doing?

JO. I'll come to the door at least.

BILL. That's a great help.

JO. And make sure you check the playground.

BILL. What would she be doing at the playground?

JO (*off-stage*). Just check the junction there anyway.

BILL (*off-stage*). Will you stop pushing me will you? Christ. I know where the front door is.

There is the sound of a door slamming shut. After a pause
JO *returns with a bowl of soup. She is upset. She puts it
down in front of* BOB.

JO. There's your soup. Go ahead. (*She sits down nervously and
watches the door.* BOB *eats.*) That's easy to make as well.
(*Beat.*) I can't imagine where she's got to. (*Beat.*) It doesn't
take many brains . . . (*Beat.*) And you're so right about the
roads as well. (*Pause.*) If something's happened to her.
(*Pause.*) Was she alright in the van on the way up?

BOB. O aye.

JO. I should've told Bill to check the station. And the carpark.
Maybe the cinema too. (*Pause.*) She didn't say anything at
all?

BOB. What about?

JO. I don't know. Her life. How's she feeling? Has she been
under a lot of stress perhaps?

BOB. Stress?

JO. With work.

BOB. I couldnae say.

JO. Maybe that's why she's leaving her job. It can be very
difficult you know. You start with all these expectations
about the good work you're going to do but really the
reality of it, the day to day reality of it, seeing people sick
and dying, it gets to you, it really gets to you, you wouldn't
be human if it didn't get to you. And it can get so as, with
everything else, you just feel, so alone, so desperately alone
as though that's all there is in the world, sickness and illness,
that there's no life in it at all, and you just want to . . .
disappear from that world completely. Maybe that's what
happened to her.

Silence.

BOB (*as though just occurring*). Jesus mothering fuck.

JO. What?

BOB. I've just remembered.

JO. Yes?

BOB. She's got my van keys in her bag.

JO. Oh Bob. My heart. You shouldn't bother about that.

BOB. I'm no bothered.

JO. That's the least of our worries.

BOB. It's not my van. (*Continuing eating.*)

JO. A van. Just now. With Katie . . . Oh Katie, what are you doing? Where have you gone? (*Pause.*) How's the soup?

BOB. It's a lovely soup.

JO. It's not too sweet?

BOB. It's perfectly balanced.

JO. Bill likes it sweet. You've got to use the . . . (*The doorbell rings.*) Oh thank God. (*Getting up.*) That'll be her there now. A lot of fuss over nothing. I'm just coming . . . one minute . . . I'm on my way . . .

She quickly leaves the room. BOB *gets up and takes his cigarettes out of his jacket pocket. He scratches his face and neck. He looks for an ashtray. He walks over and has a look out of the patio windows. It is pitch black outside. He picks up a piece of the decorative, golden fruit, puts it back, etc.*

VIV (*off-stage*). When did your sofas come?

JO (*off-stage*). Three days ago.

VIV (*off-stage*). You had some wait for them.

CHRIS (*off-stage*). Where was your Bill off to in such a hurry, Jo?

JO (*off-stage*). Four months. Nowhere as such he's/

VIV (*off-stage*). They so suit the room.

CHRIS (*off-stage*). Very nice.

VIV (*off-stage*). You have to have a tidy room with that sort of furniture. It wouldn't last five minutes in my place without one of they boys creating havoc.

BOB *puts on his jacket and goes out the patio doors.*

CHRIS (*off-stage*). Where are the old ones?

JO (*off-stage*). Bill put them in one of his units.

VIV (*off-stage*). You must have enough for another houseful in they units.

BOB *disappears into the darkness.* CHRIS *and* VIV *enter like a storm. Even though they are loud their clothes aren't, they are both very well-dressed, tasteful, well-groomed, they exude the effort of appearance.* VIV *is a little heavy, but only slightly, she wears leather trousers, a pink mohair jumper and a darker pink scarf. She has half-a-dozen or so women's magazines (*Cosmopolitan, *etc.)* . CHRIS *is taller and slimmer, almost lanky. They continually tease each other and 'clown' about.*

VIV. Feel free to give some of it to us.

CHRIS. What's the occasion?

JO (*off-stage*). What for?

CHRIS. Dinner?

JO (*off-stage*). It was Katie's idea. She said she wanted to come over, she said she had something important to say, I don't know what, I suppose something to do with her and Bob but for some reason she's . . .

On 'Bob', JO *enters the room, holding a baked potato. Naturally, she is surprised not to see him.*

JO. Oh.

CHRIS. What are you doing with that potato Jo?

JO. I'm not doing anything.

CHRIS. An' a bowl of soup as well.

VIV. You poor wee soul.

JO. That's not my plate.

VIV. Given up on your guests. Alone out here with a prisoner's dinner of soup and tatties.

CHRIS. Never mind Jo, me and Viv are here now.

VIV. And I brought you some old magazines as well to read.

CHRIS. We'll keep you company.

VIV. There's an article here about veins in there and one about digestion in here. I've folded the pages over. And look at this one, I saw it an' immediately thought of you, see, a nice we sensitive piece on . . . wait . . . there. Look, by a psychologist or something who specialises in bereavement.

JO. Oh.

VIV. I know he's a paki but I swear by him/

JO. I'll read it later.

VIV. My migraines have gone and my bowels have cleared.

JO. Can you just leave it there.

    JO *puts the plate down and goes to the patio window.*

VIV. Suit yourself snappy. (VIV *puts the magazines on the table.*) Oh! That's a lovely table. Did you do it yersel?

JO (*distracted*). Uhuh.

VIV. What trouble yiv gone to.

CHRIS. Wee place cards as well. Is that your handwriting Jo?

JO. Uhuh.

VIV. O aye, they're very good. Italics you call that.

CHRIS. Calligraphy.

VIV. But it's italics as well Chris, when it's all slanted like that. (*To* JO.) You always were artistic. I should get you to do ma Christmas cards. Usually takes me days – my family, his family, the girls at work, the boy's friends at school, old friends, school friends, work friends, so many people, I tell you, I spent half our holiday doing postcards to all they people. Jo? Are we not here or something?

JO. Of course you are.

VIV. Staring out the window. You haven't seen us for two whole weeks. You haven't even asked us about Florida.

CHRIS. Aye. Florida.

JO. I was just about to.

VIV (*taking a chair to* JO *and placing her in it*). Well sit down then. There. And we'll tell you about Florida.

CHRIS. Florida . . .

VIV. Jo.

CHRIS. . . . was lovely.

VIV. Great service.

CHRIS. Very professional.

VIV. Very polished.

CHRIS. Superb weather.

VIV. The shops/

CHRIS. Malls.

VIV. Were brilliant.

CHRIS. Like palaces.

VIV. Cathedrals.

CHRIS. Lovely and peaceful.

VIV (*beat, then slower*). Everyone treats you like you're special.

CHRIS. No problems parking.

VIV. Just something about the place, you can't explain.

CHRIS. And inside . . .

VIV. . . . ev-ray-thing you could want.

CHRIS. You've got to be there.

VIV. Aye. (*Pointing to skirt.*) I got this.

CHRIS (*pointing to tie*). I got this.

VIV. Aye, meet Mr 'I'm so fashionable'.

CHRIS (*pointing to shirt*). And this.

VIV. It goes with everything.

CHRIS. It does not.

VIV. What would you know?

CHRIS. I've got green, I've got blue, I've got black, I've got cream.

VIV. You should've been a woman. Do you like this? (*Shows a watch.*) Look.

JO. It's very nice.

CHRIS (*seriously*). How much d'you think that cost?

JO. I don't know. A lot?

CHRIS. Have a guess.

VIV. A guess.

CHRIS. Shot in the dark.

JO. Three hundred pounds.

VIV (*slowly*). Five hundred.

CHRIS. Pounds.

VIV. Jo. Here.

CHRIS. And there?

JO. Four hundred?

CHRIS. Two fifty.

VIV. One sixty in the sales.

CHRIS. And that's dollars.

VIV. Not pounds.

CHRIS. In America.

Pause for silent reflection.

JO. I have a job keeping up with you two.

VIV. Well, American sales, you've got to go a little bit mad. (*She twirls.*) But now I'm just happy to be home and I just can't wait to get back to work and be rid of this one.

CHRIS. The feeling's mutual bitch.

VIV. Don't call me bitch. (JO, *thinking they've finished, tries to get up.*) You, stay where you are. We got you something as well.

CHRIS. Brought you back a wee present.

VIV *takes something wrapped in a green paper napkin from her bag.*

JO. What's all this for?

VIV. Look at the nice shells.

JO. I wasn't expecting anything.

CHRIS. We know you like shells.

JO. I do . . .

VIV. They had food in them.

CHRIS. But originally they were from the sea.

VIV (*scathing*). I married him for his brains. (*Beat.*) We went to a lovely wee seafood restaurant.

CHRIS. Molluscs.

VIV (*to CHRIS*). Like you. (*To JO.*) In Miami.

CHRIS. Coral Grove it was.

VIV. Open air.

CHRIS. Decked floors.

VIV. And wee Cuban waiters. I hope you appreciate them Jo because I had to have three servings to get that many shells.

JO. I do, they're really lovely. Very pretty. But I . . .

VIV. They hit the spot mind.

CHRIS. It's more than a spot they have to hit.

VIV. Get away. He's always on to me to lose my three tummies and cow's arse and then he's always trying to get me to eat puddings as well. Men. What they like to look at and what they like to touch, eh! Look at him now, stop feeling your bits – you'll ruin them.

CHRIS. I wasnae feeling anything.

JO *gets up and starts for the kitchen door.*

VIV. Cannae leave them alone for a minute. Wanker. (*Mock confidential to* JO.) The other day I found him watching a porn video, the boys playing upstairs as well, and I said, 'What's that?' He said a health programme.

CHRIS. It didn't stop you watching it.

VIV. Yea, well, I've always been interested in health.

CHRIS. Especially drinking to it.

VIV. Oh aye.

CHRIS. A little bit dry in here Jo.

VIV. There's a bottle of wine in my bag.

CHRIS (*lifting a glass from the table*). Let's get the night underway.

JO. Don't use those please.

CHRIS. How no?

JO. I've set the table.

CHRIS. It doesn't bother me.

JO. We've decided to use the Venetian ones tonight.

VIV. I'm not bothered what glass I drink from.

JO. I'll get the glasses.

CHRIS. We can drink from the bottle if it bothers you that much.

JO. If you can just wait a minute.

JO *leaves, taking the potato with her.*

CHRIS. What's she like.

VIV. Probably been at it herself already. (*Beat.*) D'you know what I could do with right now?

CHRIS. What's that?

VIV. One of they Daiquiri's.

CHRIS. Oh aye.

VIV. Or a Rum Runner.

CHRIS. The rum, aye, down at the Banana Cabana especially.

VIV. You with your shirt off all tanned! (*Sadly.*) But it's fading already. (*Beat.*) Come on with the wine Jo.

CHRIS (*picking up the Venetian glass*). There's a wee drop in here.

VIV *and* CHRIS *look towards the kitchen. Behind them* BOB *returns through the patio doors.*

BOB. Alright there.

VIV. For the holy love of God.

CHRIS. Jesus Christ. (*Spilling wine down his shirt.*) O man.

VIV. Who are you?

BOB. Bob.

CHRIS. Bob? (*Wiping shirt.*) Fuck.

VIV. Katie's Bob?

BOB. Aye.

VIV. Christ.

CHRIS. Scared the living shit out o' us man.

VIV. Thought you were a ghost.

CHRIS. Coming out of the night like that!

VIV. No harm done, eh.

CHRIS. Not much anyway. (*Shaking hands.*) Jesus.

VIV. Bob then.

CHRIS. I'm Chris.

BOB. Chris.

CHRIS. This is Viv.

VIV. Bob.

BOB. Viv.

CHRIS. White as sheet now.

VIV. Aye. Fright of my life. Some entrance you make. Trying
t' kill us. (*Putting her hand to her breast.*) You got my heart
beating so fast I could hardly tell the beats apart!

She slaps him playfully on the arm.

BOB. I was only killing myself.

VIV. Is that right?

BOB. Having a smoke.

VIV. Oh aye. You're a one.

CHRIS. Sit down.

He returns to his chair, notices the magazines.

VIV. And you're Katie's special friend, then?

BOB. I don't know about that.

VIV. No need to be shy.

CHRIS. And what is it you do?

VIV. You're with friends.

BOB. I drive a van.

CHRIS. Is that right?

BOB. Aye.

CHRIS. I sell pensions myself.

BOB. Do you?

CHRIS. Aye. White collar, you know. (*Taking card from
pocket.*) Here. That's the company I work for. That's my
private line. And take that look of alarm off your face son,
I'm not going to try and sell you anything here! This is a
social occasion, you know what I mean, but I will just say
why not start having a wee think about the future, that's all,
just the future, and the uncertainty of it all. Okay. (*Clapping
his hands together firmly.*) Enough said, eh.

VIV. As always. Why not make yourself useful donkey. Go and
give Jo a hand.

CHRIS. Do I have a choice?

VIV (*ignoring him*). What are you looking at there?

BOB. A magazine.

CHRIS (*mumbling to himself as he goes*). I'll take that as a no.

BOB *continues reading.*

VIV. That's one of mine. I brought them over. All about women they are. About the fascinating and complex creatures we are. Have you found something interesting?

BOB. Nothing at all. (*Beat.*) There's an article there on tea.

Silence.

VIV. On tea!? To think someone sits in an office in London and thinks up these things! I'm a coffee person myself. I like the buzz it gives. Or a wee vodka! D'you know I used to work in an off sales in town. That would make a good article. Some of the folk you got in there! Junkies, alchy's, beggars, I could regale you with some horror stories – ask Jo. Oh, there was this one time when some smack head came in and tried to rob one o' the Saturday boys, beat him over the head with a packet of one pound coins and then stabbed him in the back nine times and then kicked him to the ground. Shocking. He's alright though now, can you believe that. Nine times in the back and plays football on a Sunday morning still! But I take it all in my stride because I know how to enjoy myself.

CHRIS *returns on 'Shocking' with a bottle and the cork screw.*

CHRIS. Has she stopped since I left?

VIV. I'm talking to Bob.

CHRIS. I need to take paracetamols just to listen to her.

VIV. But now I work for one of they call centres. I'm one of those lovely voices you hear down the phone.

CHRIS. Aye, and now the whole country's swallowing bottle fulls o' pills.

VIV. Where's Jo?

CHRIS (*starting to pour into table glasses*). She's crawling about all over the floor through there on her hands and knees.

VIV. What's she playing at now?

CHRIS. Don't ask me. Must've lost something. I'll just use these ones anyway. There you go Bob. (*Beat.*) Wait a minute. (*Pause.*) I've just realised. We're so stupid Viv! If Bob's here and Jo's in there . . . (*Looks about.*) Where's Katie then?

VIV. Oh aye.

CHRIS. Bob?

VIV. I hadn't noticed.

CHRIS. Where is she?

VIV. Is she not coming or something?

BOB. She's decided to fuck off for the night.

VIV. Fuck off? What do you mean 'Fuck off'?

BOB. She's gone.

CHRIS. Gone gone?

VIV. And just left you here?

BOB. Aye. Her old fella thinks she's away for a walk.

VIV. A walk! Where's there to walk?

BOB. This is it.

VIV. What about that. Just vanished.

BOB. So it seems.

CHRIS. Into the night.

VIV. Whatever next.

JO *returns, very discomposed, with one Venetian glass.*

JO. And now one of my Venetian glasses is missing as well. This isn't happening to me. Tonight of all nights. I've had those glasses for years. For years. I'm sure it's not in here. (*Seeing* BOB.) Bob. (*Beat.*) There you are.

VIV. Of course he's here.

JO. I thought you'd/

VIV. Where else would he be?

JO. I'd absolutely no idea. Where did you go?

BOB. I was in your garden there.

VIV. You never said how fit young Bob here was?

JO. I thought you'd gone as well.

VIV. Or how young.

JO. But you're here.

VIV. Lucky Katie.

CHRIS. Aye Jo, why didn't you say anything about Katie.

JO. Katie. Yes, I know. I was going to but then . . . Bob . . .
I really thought she'd be back any minute. Bill's out looking
for her now. I just tried to phone him but I can never get
through. I don't know where she might be.

VIV. Come on Jo, you know her as well as me.

JO. What?

VIV. She's just a nasty piece of goods.

JO. Viv, please.

VIV. Disappearing. What sort of behaviour's that? It's just
childish. That woman's never grown up. Women like her
don't have to. She even dresses like a teenager.

CHRIS. She's got a good figure.

VIV. Who asked you. (*To* BOB.) I think she's too skinny
myself. Little skirts and bright shirts and you know Jo what
she had on the other week when I saw her.

JO. You saw her?

VIV. For a coffee and a chat, didn't I say?

JO. No.

VIV. We often meet up for a coffee in Princes Square. Just
before I went away. She wanted to talk about Florida.

JO. Florida?

VIV. Aye. Florida.

JO. She's not interested in Florida.

VIV. She had enough questions she wanted answering for someone who's not interested. But she had on an ankle bracelet, no, believe me, I saw it, very fine gold, dangling there, loosely, and a black patent stiletto balancing on her toes. I don't know, but I think it's tartish. Even if it is Cartier.

JO. Cartier?

VIV. Don't ask me how she affords it. Unless you've been buying her expensive gifts.

BOB. On what I get?

VIV (*profoundly*). Your youth is your wealth.

JO. I think we should stop talking about her like this.

VIV. You won't ever hear a word against her.

JO. Not at this minute in time no, I won't.

CHRIS. Aye, that's right. For myself Bob, I don't think it matters very much what she wears or if she's got an ankle bracelet from Cartier at all, okay? That woman's always immaculately turned out in my book.

VIV. Of course it doesn't matter as such, we can see past that. I'm just saying what other people might think who don't know her, okay, I'm not the enemy here.

JO. She's been a good friend to me over the years. She's been very supportive and generous. And not just to me. To Bill as well.

VIV. She's not got the same commitments as me. She can afford to be supportive if that's what you want to call it.

JO. Call what?

VIV (*piqued*). Call anything Jo, I'm fucked if I care, and to be perfectly frank I'm fed up hearing about her. The life she has. You wouldn't see her in the shopping centre pushing a baby in a chair with a stick of a husband pushing an old mother in another.

CHRIS (*prods her*). Oi.

VIV (*continuing*). Get off.

CHRIS. That's my Mum.

VIV. You had to come from somewhere I suppose. (*Beat.*) I wish I could just think of myself and meet a nice young man at my age and then just disappear into the middle of nowhere. But I wouldn't dare do such a thing. Especially when you've gone to all this trouble, making a lovely meal for us all. (*Points to salad bowl.*) What is that in there anyway?

JO. It's an avocado salad.

VIV. I like loads and loads of vegetables Jo but I'm telling you now I can't stand avocados. And what are they tiny wee ball things?

JO. Couscous.

VIV. I don't think I like them either.

JO. Well why don't I just put everything away. You know, nothing's working out. Forget even trying to have dinner now at all. First Katie, then Bob, then my glass . . . I only wanted us all to have a nice evening together.

VIV. We are having a nice evening together.

JO. For something to go right.

VIV. It's only a glass.

JO. It's not . . . Viv, you know it's not only a glass. The whole night's a complete disaster. (*Beat.*) We haven't enjoyed ourselves for ages, have we, the three of us? (*To* CHRIS.) And you. (*Beat.*) But us three girls. I can't remember when we last had a good time and I know it's been because of me but . . .

VIV. It's not just because of you.

JO. But I don't want to just sit here. Especially this time of year. (*Pause.*) April should be a happy month. The winter's past, the cold is over and gone, the daffodils cover the earth and the new buds appear on the trees. Everything begins again and it's a real wonder. (*Pause.*) I used to love the spring. But now when the days start to get longer and I see the light coming through the windows in the morning I just think well that's another year gone and I'm still here. (*Pause.*) It's been two, sorry three, time's a mess, three springs since Sam died and I'm still here. I wonder why I'm still here. (*Pause.*) I've got to do something. I don't know what to do though. I just sit here and look and think 'now what?' It's just this nothingness, literally nothingness. It's driving me nuts. My life is passing me by. (*Pause.*) Anyway, I'm not having a moan. I'm just, I'm so bored, (*Laughing.*) I'm just so bored, that's all. I've got to do something. (*Frightened.*) I don't know what to do. (*Silence.*) You know, I just keep Sam's bedroom door closed all the time and pretend he's in there sleeping.

Silence.

VIV. Oh Jo.

JO. And now Katie. (*Beat.*) I hate to think of her out there. You know, I'm really scared something terrible's happened to her as well. It's perfectly possible. My dear, dear friend. She's been such a good friend to me over the years. (*Beat.*) Where is she?

VIV. Well, I tell you, you can let her ruin your night but she's not going to ruin mine and you shouldn't let her ruin yours either Jo.

CHRIS. Come on with you. Shut up and have a laugh.

VIV. Aye.

JO. Maybe you're right.

VIV. Of course I am.

JO. I shouldn't get worked up anymore.

VIV. Good.

JO. It's probably over nothing.

VIV. Aye.

JO. We're here to enjoy ourselves.

CHRIS. This it is.

JO. It's not as if I like having my stomach churning!

VIV. Absolutely.

JO. And I might just have a little drink.

VIV. You do that Jo.

JO. To hell with it, you know, to absolute hell with it all.

CHRIS. And you know what else you need Jo?

JO. What's that? (*Taking glass from table.*) Just to relax.

CHRIS. A bit of Chris's magic.

VIV. Magic?

JO. I don't think/

CHRIS. Wait.

VIV (*pouring JO a drink*). Look at him. What magic do you know?

CHRIS. Not magic magic. Jo, this'll cheer you up. Listen. See if you can get it. You have to listen carefully now. Okay? Right. How many animals was it that Moses took on the ark?

JO. The ark?

CHRIS. Aye.

JO. Two of each.

CHRIS. Are you sure?

JO. Yes, two. Everyone knows that.

CHRIS. Two. No Jo. See. None. You weren't paying attention. Moses didn't take any animals on the ark. That was Noah.

JO. Oh, yes.

CHRIS. Come on. Noah's ark.

JO (*drinking quickly and emptying the glass*). I wasn't thinking.

CHRIS. Clearly.

JO. I've never been good at these.

CHRIS. You have to be quick.

He laughs loudly. JO *joins in, forcing a laugh.*

JO. It's very funny. It's very good.

VIV. I don't see the point of it. He did the same one on me.

CHRIS. It makes you look stupid.

VIV. It's not magic though.

JO (*forcing herself*). But it's funny Viv, it's very funny. You're such a funny man Chris.

CHRIS. That's it. Next seen in the Theatre Royal, Bath Street. Name in lights. (*Singing.*) The animals went in two by two . . .

VIV *slaps him playfully.* JO *has stopped laughing.*

VIV. That's just him constantly. Full of carry on.

CHRIS. . . . hurrah, hurrah. The animals went in two . . .

VIV (*firmly*). Doesn't know when to stop.

CHRIS *stops.* BOB, *who has stopped reading, is the only one not laughing. He looks at* JO.

BOB. I might just go out for a smoke.

VIV. Aye, I'll join you under the gazebo Bob. Get away from this maniac.

CHRIS. You've just had one in the car.

VIV. And I'll just have another one in the garden Chris. Am I not allowed to enjoy myself when I have the chance?

CHRIS. I'm not stopping you enjoying yourself.

VIV. What are you doing then?

CHRIS. I'm not doing /

VIV. Come on Bob.

JO. I'll put the lights on.

VIV. I don't think we'll need them!

VIV and BOB go outside. BOB takes his jacket and puts it on. JO puts on the light and a well-designed patio and terrace become visible. CHRIS looks at BOB and VIV out the window.

CHRIS. Just because she can't smoke in the house she thinks she has to make up for it when we're out. You should've seen her on holiday. I like to get nice drunk but not so totally paralytic you can't stand up. (*Beat.*) She was just pure staggering everywhere. (*Beat.*) Spent half the time in bed.

VIV is seen laughing and flirting with BOB as they drift off further out of the light.

He's a young-looking lad, isn't he?

JO (*quietly*). He's only a boy.

CHRIS. What's Katie doing with him?

JO. I don't know.

CHRIS. Doesn't seem her type.

JO. Maybe's she's lonely.

CHRIS. Lonely!? Her. When she's ever lonely. I don't know about lonely Jo, you know what I mean. (*Beat.*) I've not aged that much since I was his age I think I'm still in pretty good shape for my age. Wait and see what he's like in a few years' time, sitting in a van all day, aye, reading the paper, listening to the radio, eating chips, the life ahead of him, see then what he's like. Aye. The poor sod.

As CHRIS looks out the window JO turns as though hearing a noise off stage. She walks to the dining room door. CHRIS continues to watch as outside BOB and VIV disappear.

JO. Katie? (*Pause.*) Katie? (*Beat.*) Is that you?

BILL (*off-stage*) It's me?

JO. Bill?

BILL (*enters*). Aye.

JO. Is Katie with you?

BILL. No.

JO. Did you see her?

BILL. No, I saw nothing, no-one.

JO. What are you doing back then?

BILL (*shaking hands*). Hello Chris.

CHRIS. Alright pal.

JO. And you're soaked through.

CHRIS. Did you have the roof down on your car?

BILL. No.

JO. Look at you.

BILL. Get off me.

JO. Where's your coat?

BILL. By the door. (*Pointing to glass.*) What are you doing with that?

JO (*putting glass down*). I'm not doing anything with it. Were the roads wet?

BILL. No, they're as dry as sand. (*Under his breath.*) Like yourself clearly.

CHRIS. It's torrential Bill.

BILL. Aye. Sarcasm Chris.

JO. If she'd just gone out for a walk you would've seen her.

BILL. It's a big place Jo. I'm going straight back out.

CHRIS. Have a quick drink first Bill.

BILL. I'd rather get it done and sit down for the night.

CHRIS. Stay where you are a minute.

BILL. I'm off the drink Chris.

CHRIS. Since when?

BILL. Since now.

CHRIS. Why's that?

BILL. What?

CHRIS. The drink?

JO. You're supposed to be looking Bill.

BILL. I'm saying hello to Chris okay. (*Beat.*) You can always go out and have a look yourself Jo. You know, if it's that urgent.

JO. I would if I could.

He holds out his car keys for her.

BILL. Go on then.

JO. That's not fair.

She goes to sit in the chair at the back.

BILL. The only thing outside the door for her is death and damnation.

JO (*quietly*). You would've seen her.

BILL. Aye, that's right, sit down away fay us.

JO. If she was okay.

BILL (*beat*). What was it you were saying?

CHRIS. Er, eh, why you're off the drink?

BILL. I'm starting to get a gut.

CHRIS. A gut?

BILL. Aye.

CHRIS. For fuck's sake, you're built like a racing snake.

BILL. An' I intend to stay that way. (*Beat.*) Give us a wee splash. Wet my mouth. Was that your new car outside?

CHRIS. It is, aye.

BILL. Not bad.

CHRIS. A nice motor.

BILL. Good runner?

CHRIS. For a family car. (*Giving glass.*) Cheers.

BILL. Ta. How much did you pay for that? About five grand?

CHRIS. Don't be so ridiculous. For an R reg Merc.

BILL. I didn't see the reg.

CHRIS. Full spec. Alloys. Air con. Leather trim.

BILL. As standard?

CHRIS. As standard? Fuck! There's nothing standard about that motor.

JO (*timid, whilst still seated*). Bill?

BILL. Did you hear something?

CHRIS (*joking*). Aye, a wee whisper.

JO. Are we just going to sit here then and wait for a knock on the door? Is that what we're going to do. Just sit here. Wait for a knock. She might be on the roads.

BILL (*indifferent*). She might be, aye.

JO. And been in an accident.

BILL. People walk up and down them roads everyday without having an accident.

JO. I know they do.

BILL. Well then. (*Beat and ignoring* JO.) And a good drive is it, the Merc?

CHRIS. Sweet as a nut.

JO. But not everyone does.

BILL. Not a bit heavy on the steering.

CHRIS. Not at all.

JO. Not everyone's that lucky.

BILL. That's what I heard.

CHRIS. Where did you hear that?

JO. Some people still have accidents Bill.

BILL (*very impatient*). I know people still have accidents. But not everyone. Not every time they go outside. (*Pause.*)

Christ. This may come as a surprise to you Jo, but most people go outside every day without having a fucking accident. Alright.

CHRIS. Bill.

BILL. What?

CHRIS. Easy.

BILL. Me? You try living with her pal. It's constant. Constant.

Short pause.

JO (*quietly*). I still might just phone the police all the same.

BILL. Christ alive.

JO. Just to make sure.

BILL. You'll sit down and phone no one.

Silence.

BILL. Can you see what I've got to live with? What can you do with her? (*To* JO.) Just let it alone, eh, please, because you're killing me with this Jo. (*Beat.*) Every single day. (*Behind,* BOB, *holding a letter, and* VIV *emerge from the dark.*) Aye, no, that's right, steering, your car, I read it in some magazine, your car, heavy on the steering, seemingly. But it's not then?

CHRIS. No, no, not so as you'd notice.

BILL. Well, as long as it drives alright. (*Beat.*) Is that Viv there?

CHRIS. And her new pal. Drives beautifully.

BILL. That's what's important then.

VIV (*coming in from the patio with* BOB). Hello people.

BILL. Hello Viv.

VIV. Bill. (*Beat.*) What's Jo doing over there?

BILL. Her usual thing.

VIV. Jo? That's the end of that little mystery.

CHRIS. What mystery?

VIV (*hitting him*). Katie yi eejit. (*Beat.*) Jo. Katie's left Bob here a wee letter. Show them Bob.

JO. A letter?

BOB. More of a note actually.

CHRIS (*eagerly*). A suicide note!

VIV. No, not a suicide note yi div. (*Consoling* BOB.) Don't listen to him.

CHRIS. Christ!

VIV. Just a few words is all.

JO. A letter.

BILL. What does it say then?

JO (*going for letter*). Does it say where she's gone?

VIV. After a fashion.

JO. It must! Can I see it? This must be what she wanted to tell us. It must say where she's gone. (*Taking the letter.*) Oh what a blessed relief. Give it to me. Give it to me and I'll read it.

Blackout.

ACT THREE

Bedroom with an en suite bathroom stage left. Glass topped dressing table next to bathroom door. A double bed, centre, stool at the end of the bed, decorative quilted coat hangers on wardrobe door to stage right, wax candles in glass holders wrapped with ribbons, neatly folded towels on the bed. Again the room is immaculate, decorated largely in white, except for photographs on the dressing table which are disturbed. One photograph is on the floor.

BILL, *sitting on the end of the bed, begins to undress out of his wet shirt and then dry himself with a towel. He discards his clothes on the floor and as he does so he comes across* KATIE*'s black coat, also on the floor.* CHRIS *lingers at the door to the en suite, holding a bottle of aftershave.*

BILL. He was from Florida.

CHRIS. Florida?

BILL. Aye, Florida.

CHRIS. I've no recollection of that.

BILL. You must remember him.

CHRIS. I don't remember him at all.

BILL. In the sauna.

CHRIS. Not a thing.

BILL. You must.

CHRIS. 'Fraid not. *(Sprays aftershave.)* This is quite nice.

BILL. He was talking about his condominium.

CHRIS. Is it an aftershave or Eau de Cologne?

BILL. Or condos as they call them over there.

CHRIS. It'll say on the box.

BILL. You know, new places, like these ones here only nicer.

CHRIS *exits into the en suite.* BILL *remains sitting on the end of the bed. He looks at the black coat.*

I can't believe you don't remember him.

CHRIS (*off-stage*). Who?

BILL (*impatient*). That man. He was in construction. (*Beat.*) You better not be snooping about in there Chris.

CHRIS (*coming to the door*). I'm looking at your skincare range.

BILL. Don't interfere with my things alright.

CHRIS. Looks like someone already has though pal.

BILL. What?

CHRIS. There's something on the floor there.

BILL. Where?

CHRIS (*pointing at the coat and going back into the en suite*). There.

BILL. Oh aye.

CHRIS. On the floor.

BILL. So there is. O aye. Don't you worry about that. (*As* BILL *now talks he goes to the coat, lifts it up and cautiously looks in the pockets. Whilst he speaks he finds a passport.*) Anyway, he was saying living out there was outstanding. He bought a place for a hundred and twenty thousand dollars. Easily affordable. Four bedrooms and a swimming pool. After what I paid for this. He's semi-retired; golf, gardening, sitting outside all year round with his wife and kids, grand-children over for holidays as well. It must be fantastic. None of this crap.

CHRIS (*off-stage*). You've got a lovely place here Bill, what are you talking about, crap?

BILL. Aye, I know I've got a nice place here. I don't need to be told. But it's not ideal. Some of the houses never got

built and the ones that did are not without their problems.
There's been much . . . there's been other problems as well.
(*Beat.*) And you know as well as me the only heat we get
here is sitting in a pine box in a David Lloyd Sports Centre.
That's far from ideal. Do you think that's what I work all
the days and weeks of my life for? To sit in a pine box.
I could've got that back in Govan when I was a lad. I didn't
have to move out here for that. I don't have to spend twelve
hours a day in a PortaCabin in Rutherglen or Motherwell
or the Mearns for that. I could've stayed in Govan and got
a concession pass to the local gym with all my pals from
school if I didn't want to have nothing to show for my
industry. Or my labour. Or my ambition. (*He hangs the
coat up on the door.*) I've built me up a massive business.
I've made me good profits. I've bought this house outright.
I've got as much as that man only you just have to look at
him to see what he's achieved. A nice place in Florida.
Swimming pool and garden. Family over for holidays. What
have I to show for my grief? (*Pause.*) I thought that was
your intention in going out there for your holidays in the
first place, because you were impressed by what he'd said.
Chris? Did it confirm what he was saying in all?

CHRIS (*off-stage*). I've no idea pal. The only reason we went
to Florida was 'cos the kids wanted to see Mickey Mouse.

BILL. Mickey Mouse!? Thanks for listening pal. (*Sharply.*)
What are you doing in there anyway all this time?

CHRIS. With you in a minute.

BILL *goes to the toilet doorway.*

BILL. Are you shitting in there? (*Looks in the bathroom.*) For
fuck's sake man.

CHRIS (*coming to the doorway*). Just a wee one.

BILL (*outraged*). I don't care what size it is. (*Very affronted.*)
That's my toilet, that's where I shit. Jo doesn't even shit
there.

BILL *manhandles* CHRIS *towards the door.*

CHRIS. Alright Bill, it was only a shit.

BILL. Shit in the hall you fucking muppet. Do you not think I haven't got enough t' contend with, eh, with her downstairs.

CHRIS. Okay.

BILL. And her infernal questions.

CHRIS. Alright.

BILL. I came up here for some quiet.

CHRIS. Okay. I'll just sit here. (*Beat.*) Quietly then. (*Beat.*) Stay out of your way. (*Beat.*) Not say anything. Even though, I think Jo's got a wee point . . .

BILL. Don't you start defending her.

CHRIS. I'm not defending her but I can see where she's coming from.

BILL. Chris.

CHRIS. That letter's only added to the confusion.

BILL. I'm not asking you now.

CHRIS. But if someone . . . Okay. I'm quiet. Aye. (*Silence.* BILL *continues to change.* CHRIS *continues smelling himself.*) I wish I'd bought some of this when I was on my holidays. It's an Eau de Cologne by the way. I found the box. I could've got it duty free. Save myself a tenner or so but the kids always want something first, you know. And I like that tie. That's a nice tie. Jo get you that?

BILL. No, Katie.

CHRIS. Katie?

BILL. Aye, just for Christmas once.

CHRIS. That's very nice. (*Looking at the label then the tie proper.*) That's Hermes you know.

BILL. Get off.

CHRIS. Where'd she get that in Glasgow? Fraser's or somewhere?

BILL. Aye, I think so. Are you finished now?

CHRIS. Very nice. (*Beat.*) Do you know Eau de Cologne means 'water of Cologne', Cologne being a place in France.

BILL. It means toilet water.

CHRIS. No, I have a smattering of French and literally it means/

BILL. Literally nothing Chris. It's a word. It means what it is. Toilet water. Alright. It's not something that's open to your negotiation.

CHRIS. Aye well, whatever it means it settles into a really nice smell. Do you use it much yourself?

BILL. Now and then.

CHRIS. Do you!? I don't think I've ever smelt it on you.

BILL. Is that right?

CHRIS. I'd know if I had. It's such a distinctive aroma. It's a shame if it's just sitting there on the shelf because after a while it starts to evaporate and then/

BILL. Och for fuck's sake.

CHRIS (*innocently*). What?

BILL. What!? Christ. Yir as subtle as a brick.

BILL *roughly pulls a suitcase from under the bed* (*stage left side*). *He opens it and looks inside – it is full of baby clothes. He falls quiet for a moment and quickly closes it and pulls out another suitcase. It is full of gift type things – ties, shirts, socks, aftershaves. He removes a bottle of the same aftershave.* CHRIS *looks over his shoulder.*

CHRIS (*astonishment*). Fuckin' Ali Baba.

BILL. Here.

CHRIS. What a treasure trove.

BILL. Take it and shut up about it.

CHRIS. I don't want that.

BILL. Of course you don't.

CHRIS. I don't.

BILL. You're going on enough about it.

CHRIS. I'm only making conversation.

BILL. Have it, I'm no going to use it.

CHRIS. Aye you will.

BILL. I've got gallons of the stuff. Jo's forever buying things from catalogues. Keeps them in business. Go on. (*Beat.*) Will you just take it. (*Genuinely.*) I'd like you to have it.

CHRIS *takes the bottle.* BILL *zips up the case.*

CHRIS. Well, ta very much. You've no got anything else in there you want rid of?

BILL. Away wi yi.

CHRIS. Come on.

BILL. You're a chancer yi know that.

CHRIS. You've got to have some cheek in this life.

BILL. Aye, I suppose so. (*Beat.*) Go on then.

CHRIS. Yi wee dancer.

BILL. Help yourself.

VIV *enters.* CHRIS *delves in.*

VIV. What are you two boys up to?

BILL. We're just having a minute.

VIV. Jo's getting a bit tetchy.

BILL. What's new there.

VIV. She told me to tell you the roast's all dried out.

BILL. What's the hurry then.

VIV. And that poor wee soul's sitting down there as well.

CHRIS. Will you shut up about him.

VIV. What? The boy's been done up like a kipper. Left sat down there. In a strange house. Not knowing anyone. Utterly humiliated. Fear't about his van. His job. Not able to get a word in edgeways.

CHRIS. Alright Viv, my heart's bleeding all over the floor.

VIV. No need to be insensitive. And to top everything off Jo can't find one iota of sense in that letter.

BILL. It was clear enough.

VIV. It says very little.

BILL. It says enough.

VIV. Just apologising to Bob for using him like that.

CHRIS. Like what?

VIV. Well, that's exactly what we don't know Chris.

BILL. It says she wants to start a new life.

VIV. Aye, but why just go like that?

BILL. It's perfectly understandable.

VIV. Not to Jo it's not. She doesn't understand any of it. She's losing the place. She's pure flipping out. It's frightening to watch. What's really grating her is the fact that Katie didn't tell her anything at all. She's even gone and got her Venice bag out trying to prove to Bob what good friend's her and Katie are. I don't know what delusions she's living under and it doesn't take a brain surgeon to work out why either.

BILL. Why what?

VIV. Why Katie's gone like that.

BILL. And why is that?

CHRIS (*with sudden delight, still looking in the case*). Oh! Can I have this one? (*Showing a tie.*)

BILL. Help yourself.

CHRIS. Cheers pal.

BILL. Viv?

CHRIS. It's lovely.

VIV. What?

BILL. Why?

VIV. Why what?

CHRIS. A hundred per cent pure silk. (*New tie fastened over existing tie.*) How does it look?

VIV. Very nice. (*Beat.*) Where's all this consideration coming from Bill?

BILL. It's coming from nowhere.

CHRIS. He gave me this in all.

VIV. Did he?

CHRIS. Smell that.

VIV. Smell you! (*Takes the bottle.*) This is Chris putting on aftershave Bill. Look. Soaks himself in the stuff.

VIV *pretends to spray, with Sssshhh noises, various parts of her anatomy – her neck, armpits, knees, feet.*

CHRIS (*reclaiming bottle*). You missed a bit. (*He sprays her crotch.*)

VIV. Hey, that'll damage my ovaries.

CHRIS. Get away.

VIV *pushes* CHRIS *away but he grabs her and starts to tickle her. They fall onto the bed, thoroughly messing it up.*

VIV. Stop it. Don't.

CHRIS. You love it.

VIV. I'll wet myself. Chris (*Shrill.*) Chris.

CHRIS *stops immediately. As* VIV *gets up he tries to kiss her.*

Don't kiss my ear. (*To* BILL.) God save us, eh? (*Goes to pick up coat.*) What's this?

BILL. Just leave it.

VIV. I came up here to get away from the madness. I wish I was back on my holiday Bill. Lying on the beach.

BILL. Oh aye.

VIV. Soaking up the sun. Like the tan?

BILL (*flatly*). Fantastic.

VIV. The work I put into it.

BILL. It was a nice holiday then?

CHRIS. She wanted to live there.

VIV. I just might do that.

CHRIS. I wish you would.

VIV. It was so lovely. Except for all they wiry wee waifs on the beach. They didn't bother that one there. (*Teasing.*) Do you like that sort of woman Bill?

BILL. What sort?

VIV. The skinny sort.

BILL. No more than any other.

VIV. Oh, I thought you did. I thought you had a preference for that sort. But them aside I could move out there tomorrow. Florida. You know what's so nice about it, it doesn't matter what you've read or heard or seen on the TV, what's nice is that it exceeds all your expectations. Air conditioning everywhere. All the films first. Petrol's cheaper. Everyone speaks English, even the wee beige numbers in the restaurants.

CHRIS. They were Cubans, Viv.

VIV. Whatever. Proper food and good portions. If I had your money that's where I'd live. Get someone to run your business, sell it even, keep a wee flat in Glasgow for weddings and funerals and go and live out there. Have you ever thought of doing that? Living in Florida like that?

BILL. I'm perfectly happy where I am.

CHRIS. Oh aye!

BILL. I am.

CHRIS. We were just talking about Florida ourselves Viv.

VIV. Were you?

BILL. Not really.

CHRIS. Aye.

VIV. Seems like everyone's talking about Florida.

CHRIS. And he was saying/

BILL. Are you going to start taking pops at me as well?

CHRIS. What?

BILL. Along with her.

VIV. Me!? What am I doing?

CHRIS. I wasn't taking any pops at you Bill.

VIV. Neither was I. (*Beat.*) What's this Joehoba cream?

CHRIS. It's Johoba.

BILL. Don't mess around with Jo's things.

VIV. Och, as soon as I touch anything. She won't mind me. But it is Joehoba actually, Chris, 'cos it's Jo's hoba!

CHRIS. O aye, good one.

VIV. That's wordplay. Do you not think that's funny Bill?

BILL. Aye, it's very good.

VIV. I must tell that to Jo. Cheer her up. (*Puts cream down, sits at dressing table, uses various items.*) You need to chill out a bit as well Bill.

BILL. Aye well, I haven't just come back fay two weeks holiday. Nobody gives me five weeks off a year to chill out you know.

CHRIS. Aye well, you're your own boss.

VIV (*applying lipstick*). And we were only away for two.

BILL. Aye, I know. But you get five weeks a year.

CHRIS. When you're working, aye, five weeks seems a lot, but I've just had two weeks, and see when you've just had two weeks five weeks isn't a lot at all. That's me only got three weeks holiday left in actual fact. Just three weeks for the entire year.

BILL. I'd be glad for three weeks a year.

CHRIS. You make five times what I do. Don't you? Ten times even! Who knows. (*Pause.*) You've got money in the bank anyway. My wages are gone before I get them – pension, insurance, mortgage, car, credit cards. (*Aside to* BILL *and indicating* VIV.) And they want all the money they can get off o' you and they don't want to do a thing.

BILL. That's just the way it is.

CHRIS. This is it. (*Resuming.*) Aye, five weeks, weekends and Bank holidays. (*With pathos.*) That's not enough time to clear out the garage. I don't know when I'm ever going to get round to doing that. I've no time to myself. I wish I could just go straight from school to retirement. Aye. Cut out the middle bit. (*He picks up a CD.*) What's this like?

BILL. Shite.

VIV. Put it on anyway.

BILL. It's a magazine freebie.

VIV. It'll liven things up.

BILL. They're live enough.

CHRIS. We've come all this way.

VIV. I'm all dolled up. (*Pouting lips.*) How does that look?

BILL. Great improvement.

VIV. Who wants to kiss me first?

BILL. She's your wife.

CHRIS. I kissed her at New Year.

VIV (*kissing* BILL). Come on. It's time to party.

BILL (*furious*). Fuck off o' me Viv.

VIV. It's only a kiss.

BILL. What is it with you? (*Wiping cheek.*) Christ, that's lipstick on my face.

VIV. Steady on Bill.

BILL. Is that coming off.

VIV. I'm just trying to get a rise out of you.

BILL. I get enough grief from Jo casting about for things as it is. Bending my ear to infinity. She doesn't need any help

from you. Alright. Just leave things alone when you're in
my house. That goes for you too. Okay. Wash this muck off
now.

BILL *goes into the en suite.*

VIV (*unruffled*) Understood Bill. Wash away the evidence.
(*Beat.*) I thought you're going to put some music on?

CHRIS. O aye.

VIV (*going to wardrobe*). What's Jo got in here?

CHRIS (*music on*). It's a lovely wee system this.

VIV. I'll just have a quick look.

CHRIS. Look at the action on that.

VIV. Who's this?

CHRIS. Some dance band.

She begins to look through JO*'s clothes as loud, thudding
dance music plays.* CHRIS *lies on the bed.* VIV *takes
various items of clothes out, checking the labels and
holding them next to her, discarding dresses on the bed
and burying the coat.*

VIV. That's pure beat that is.

CHRIS. This is what Beethoven would write now.

VIV. Is that right?

CHRIS. Aye, no words or lyrics. Just instruments. There's no
difference. Listen. (*Turns up CD loud.*) It's got to be loud to
hear it properly.

VIV. I know, but keep it down a bit. You know what they're
like. (*Reproachful.*) Aye and you. Don't you think I didn't
hear what you said about me. If I wanted money do you
think I'd lumber myself with you. Look at these clothes!
I would've married someone like Bill.

CHRIS. He wouldn't have you.

VIV. Shut up.

CHRIS. Don't you want to talk to me now.

VIV. When do I ever want to talk to you. (*Beat. Continuing to look at dresses, throwing them onto the bed.*) What do you think she does with all these? Do you reckon she dresses up in them and has a Martini thinking she's floating about some fancy hotel foyer in Florence. I bet she does. I'd be as bad though. Imagine what I'd be like if one of ours had sneaked out to play and then the next thing I heard he was hit by a car. The sight – pure cut, pure bleeding, pure blood flowing everywhere. I shudder to think. God knows what went through her head. Crying in that bed for months. Blaming herself. Her own child. Dear God. (*Beat.*) How does this one look?

JO enters, she is purposeful. CHRIS continues to lie on the bed, VIV is at the wardrobe with various dresses on the bed, the suitcase is open on the floor, etc . . . The room is a mess.

VIV. Oh Jo, do you still fit into this?

JO. What are you doing with that?

VIV. Just having a wee look about.

JO (*distracted by mess*). They're my clothes.

CHRIS. I thought they were Bill's!

JO. All over the bed. (*Beat.*) Can you turn that racket off please.

VIV. Och, come on Jo.

JO. I can't think . . .

VIV. Get your black blood going.

JO. Don't talk like that Viv.

VIV. Like what?

JO (*firm*). Chris. (*Beat.*) You know like what. (*Beat.*) Turn it off will you.

CHRIS. Alright.

JO. Thank you.

CHRIS. You're no fun.

Fun? (*To* VIV.) I thought Bill was up here.

IV. He's in there.

JO. Still?

VIV. He's a bit touchy.

JO. Bill. (*Going to the door.*) He's touchy? (*To* VIV.) I've been pacing about downstairs, racking my brains . . . I'm going insane with this Viv. (*Knocking on door.*) Bill. Katie would tell me if she was planning something. She's my . . . Bill. I can't think why she wouldn't tell me. I know her. Of all people I know her. Bill?

BILL (*off-stage*). I'm in here.

JO. I want to ask you a question.

BILL (*off-stage*). What now.

JO. I want to know if Katie said anything . . . (*Seeing table.*) What's . . . my dressing table.

BILL (*opening door*). Go on.

JO. And my photos.

BILL. What do you want.

JO. On the floor.

BILL. Don't look at me.

JO. What's going on?

She picks up the photos, one of her and KATIE *and another of two girls in school uniforms.*

BILL. I haven't touched them.

JO. You've turned the place upside down.

BILL. Look at those two nightmares there.

VIV. And you're a real oasis of calm.

BILL. They're a pair of infants.

JO (*trying to restore order*). Someone's been touching them.

VIV. I love that picture there. How old were we then?

JO. Twelve.

VIV (*spiteful*). And that's you and Katie in Venice?

JO. And it goes there. Okay. (*She takes photo and puts it down.*) There is a right place for things in this room at least. (*To* BILL.) I spend all day trying to keep this house straight.

BILL. It's not for my benefit.

JO. And I'm sitting downstairs.

BILL. We know where you are.

JO. . . . in the midst of . . . utter disarray you know, trying to maintain a semblance of order there, and I come up here . . . you're up here for five minutes . . . just adding to the . . . Is that . . .

BILL. No.

JO. It's..

BILL. S'not.

JO. It is . . .

BILL. It's the other one.

JO (*going towards them*). For your sake it better be.

BILL. I was giving Chris something.

JO. Chris.

CHRIS. C'est un cravate.

JO. I got that for you.

BILL. I know.

JO. For Christmas.

BILL. So?

JO. So? (*Pause.*) Why don't you give him the one you're wearing if it's only 'so'?

BILL. What are you insinuating by that?

JO (*getting on her knees*). What do you think I'm insinuating.

BILL (*to* VIV). What have you been saying to her?

VIV. I haven't said anything.

BILL. I severely doubt that.

JO (*sotto voce*). Everything I get you you just shove under here.

BILL. Putting ideas into her head.

VIV. You can manage that yourself I'm sure.

JO. That's your mentality Bill. Aye. Hide everything away. Under the bed. Me in a corner. (*Aloud.*) I thought you said . . .

BILL. I haven't touched it.

JO. You're a bare faced liar Bill. I can see . . .

BILL. You can see nothing.

JO. I'm not blind.

BILL. I just . . .

JO. It's been moved..

BILL. I only . . .

JO. And opened.

BILL. Not rea/

JO. Is nothing sacred.

BILL. I didn't.

JO. Not even Sam's . . . few . . . things. (*Pause.*) That's his there. His little . . . (*Pause.*) My dear, sweet boy. (*Pause, then to* BILL.) Hasn't there been enough upset for one night?

BILL. I'm not upset.

JO (*exasperated*). Well I am. (*Pause.*) I'm trying to hold every-thing together here . . . and make some sense of things . . . and you're not . . . none of you seem very concerned. I've been downstairs, this is what I'm saying, trying to think of a reason . . . been going over and over and over it . . . I don't understand why she'd just go like that unless she's got something . . . No. She doesn't hide things from me. You see. I'm not getting anywhere with this. (*Hitting out.*) That's just it. I can't think clearly anymore. (*Beat.*) I want to sit down myself. It's exhausting. And now . . . there's his . . . and I'm . . . (*Putting Sam's case away.*) I really don't need any more of this tonight as well.

Silence.

CHRIS. Okay. Okay. Okay. Jo.

VIV. Chris.

CHRIS. It's alright. Do you know what's needed now? (*Pause.*) Eh? It's getting a bit heavy in here, you know.

VIV. Not now Chris.

CHRIS. Let me lift the mood a little. I've got a wee bit more magic in my bag. Jo, listen, I know how much you like these wee riddles. I absolutely love them. Calm you down.

Pause.

I'll take that as a green light. Now. Listen this time. Did you know that if your husband's, fuck. What is it? Wait a minute. Aye. Let me get it right in my head first before I speak, your husband . . . that's it, that if your husband's a widower in America you can marry his brother?

Silence.

Did you not know that?

Silence.

Eh Jo. Of course you didn't. How could you know that. It's not true. How can you marry your husband's brother if he's a widower Jo, you'd be dead, you know, you couldn't marry anyone, if he was a widower you'd be dead. D'you get it? Eh? Do you get it?

JO. That's very clever.

CHRIS. I wish I knew who thinks these up. (*To* BILL.) Don't you?

BILL. Aye.

JO. I'm glad you find me so amusing.

CHRIS. It's only a joke.

JO. Who's laughing?

CHRIS. Well it's not quite as good as the other one I admit but/

JO. This isn't a joke Chris.

VIV. Jo.

JO. This is my life.

VIV. Don't talk to him like that.

JO. Who else am I going to talk to.

VIV. Try him there.

>   BILL *has started to leave the bedroom.*

JO. I can't talk to him. Obviously.

VIV. I can see that.

JO. Skulking off.

VIV. It's no excuse though.

CHRIS. Aye.

VIV (*to* CHRIS). Sit down you. (*Beat.*) You're wasting your time asking him anyway.

BILL. Shut up Viv.

VIV. Why don't you ask me what I think.

BILL. Don't you start your stirring here then.

VIV. I think Jo might want to know what I think.

BILL. No she doesn't.

VIV. I'm not consulting you.

JO. I want to know what he thinks Viv.

VIV. Yeh I know . . .

JO. Not you.

VIV. . . . but even so.

JO. Not you I said.

VIV. Come on now Jo.

JO. I don't care what you think.

VIV. Now look here I'm only . . .

JO. Only what? I'm trying to talk to him. Not you. I want something from him. Not . . . (*Beat.*) What are you doing here anyway?

VIV. Eh?

JO (*letting her frustration and anger go fully at* VIV). I didn't ask you here. I don't want you here. I'm trying to talk to him not to you. Can't you see that. Does anything get through to you at all ever. Why don't you keep your idiot mouth shut for once and get out of my house. Of all the people in the world . . . here . . . (*Picking up the clothes and throwing them, the coat being caught amongst them.*) Take these and go now will you. That's all you want. That's all you ever come for.

VIV. Get off.

JO. A plague of locusts you are.

VIV. Stop throwing.

JO. Take them.

VIV. You've cracked completely.

JO. I'm giving them to you. (*Emptying case.*) That's all for you Chris . . .

VIV. I'm not . . .

JO. Have my dresses. And my clothes.

VIV. Keep your mangy old frocks.

CHRIS. We don't want them.

JO. Take them all and get out of here. (*Screaming.*) Get out. I don't want any of you near me. I don't want any of you looking at me.

Pause.

VIV. Chris.

CHRIS. Aye.

VIV. I didn't come here to be spoken to like that.

CHRIS. No.

VIV. We'll get a video and a pizza. (*Sniping at* JO.) Who'd want to look at you now anyway.

They start to leave. BILL *begins to follow behind.*

BILL. I'll see you two to the door.

CHRIS. Ta.

JO. Bill.

BILL. You'll have to excuse that little performance.

JO. Don't blank me.

CHRIS. That's alright pal.

BILL. And what do you think you're playing at?

JO. Don't try and blank me.

VIV. I'm not the one making a spectacle of myself.

BILL. In whose opinion.

JO. I won't let you blank me this time.

Pause. BILL *waits at the door as* VIV *and* CHRIS *leave.*

BILL. See yourselves out okay.

CHRIS (*off-stage*). Give us a call.

VIV (*off-stage*). Aye, and thanks for a lovely evening. I had a great time.

CHRIS *and* VIV *have left the room.*

JO. Did she say something to you?

Pause.

BILL. She's told me nothing.

JO. She must've said something.

BILL. She's not said anything.

JO. You expect me to believe that.

BILL. Believe what you want.

JO. When you talk about everything else.

BILL. Ach.

JO. You talk about our son.

BILL. Don't start with that.

JO. We've never . . .

BILL. Never?

JO. No. Never. You share that with her.

BILL. I share nothing.

JO. You won't say his name to me.

BILL. Go and bury your head.

JO. And open up with her. You're not married to her. You're married to me.

BILL. I'm aware of that fact.

JO. You haven't got a house with her.

BILL. That's right as well.

JO. You didn't lose a child with her.

BILL. Keep going.

JO (*saying it now after years*). You lost a child with me.

BILL (*replying equally*). I didn't lose any child Jo. You did.

   Silence.

JO (*breaking*). Me? (*Beat.*) Yes. (*Beat.*) And this is what comes to me. (*Pause.*) Everything's gone. (*Pause.*) Been left with nothing. There's nothing in this place. (*Pause.*) I look to you for . . . something. (*Pause.*) You give me nothing. (*Pause.*) And now. Tonight. I think . . . (*Pause and openly.*) What do you stay here for?

BILL. That's a bloody good question.

JO. Why don't you go then?

BILL (*starting to go*). I should go right enough.

JO. Do it.

BILL. Aye.

JO. Go away with that pair.

BILL. Don't worry I will.

JO. Katie'll be outside waiting for you as well. Aye. That would explain everything. No wonder she said nothing to me.

BILL (*stops*). Go to your bed Jo.

JO. No wonder. No wonder.

BILL. And wake up when you've stopped talking nonsense.

JO. Go and be with her.

BILL. Oh aye.

JO. I'm sure she'll make you happy.

BILL. I should leave you alright.

JO. Go on then.

BILL. I'll go.

JO. Good.

> BILL *goes to the doorway.*

(*With real fear.*) Bill. You're not . . . Bill? Please. (BILL *stops in the doorway, unseen by* JO.) I don't want to be left alone. Everything leaves me. What's wrong with me? I can't hold onto anything. My life's slipping away and I can't do anything to stop it. (*Pause.*) Bill? You're not really going. Wait. (*She gets up and starts to collect the clothes.*) I'll clear up and come down. Bill? Give me . . . Please. She's not really outside. I'm just . . . I was only . . . Bill? . . . (*She notices the coat.*) . . . I didn't mean . . . what's . . . I wasn't . . . (*Pause.*) This . . . isn't . . . (*She holds out the coat.*) Bill? Are you still there?

> *Blackout.*

ACT FOUR

Living room. KATIE's black coat is over the chair in the far corner, a purse and a passport wallet on the seat, television on, BOB, wearing his jacket, has dropped off. A brown paper bag is on the coffee table, tickets and stubs and brochures spill out of it. JO comes in with some tea, puts it on the coffee table, looks at BOB, no response, then the door and then returns to the kitchen. BILL enters. He looks at BOB and the tea and then in the direction of the kitchen. The kitchen door is ajar (although we cannot see in). BILL looks at the coat and the kitchen door.

BILL. There's some tea there for you.

BOB. What's that?

BILL. Some tea.

BOB. Tea.

BILL. There.

BOB. Ta. (*Drinks the tea, much relieved, sits back.*) I usually have two cups before I go to work. I have one when I get to work. That's three. Then elevenses, that's four. A cup at lunchtime, then one in the afternoon. Five, six. One when I get home. Two with dinner and then one before my bed. Ten in all. (*Drinks.*)

Silence.

BILL. Well, fascinating as that is son I've been on the phone to the station. The last train's at 11.27. The next one's not till half five in the morning. Alright?

BOB. Aye.

BILL. Get the 11.27.

BOB. Whatever you say pal.

BILL. Aye. (*Pause.*) Best get that then.

BILL *sits down.*

BOB. I'll no be home before I'm back up here again.

BILL. How's that?

BOB. You won't want that old van outside your house for long.

BILL. Don't worry about your van.

BOB. Worry, I tell you, they don't pay me enough to worry.

BILL. Is that right.

BOB. The money's shite.

BILL. Is it?

BOB. Oh, it's shite. Working from seven o'clock to whenever o'clock.

BILL. I'm sure there's something else you can do.

BOB. Me? No. Nothing pal. Not a thing. Absolutely fuckin' nothing.

Silence. JO *comes in with some sandwiches. No acknowledgement from* BILL. *She puts them on the coffee table.*

JO. Will those sandwiches be okay?

BOB. Oh aye.

BILL. I don't think we've got time for sandwiches.

JO (*to* BOB). I can do some more.

BILL. There's enough there.

JO. It wouldn't have been right to eat dinner. Just the three of us.

BILL (*under his breath*). No it wouldn't.

BOB. I'll get on with these.

JO (*to* BILL). What about you? (*Pause.*) Bill? Do you want a sandwich? Bill?

BILL *ignores her. Silence.* JO *leaves.*

BILL. Ten cups a day you were saying.

BOB. This is it.

BILL. You must have some bladder.

BOB. Especially as tea's a diuretic.

BILL. What's that then?

BOB. Makes you piss.

BILL. Is that right?

BOB (*pointing out the magazine*). So the magazine was saying.

BILL. I didn't know that.

BOB. In there.

BILL. Diuretic.

BOB. A whole article on tea.

BILL. That's a new word for me.

Silence. BILL picks up the magazine and starts to look through it. BOB eats his sandwiches. JO returns with a vase with the daffodils. She puts it on the window ledge, centres it.

JO. How does that look there?

BILL. Don't you think you should give Viv and Chris them back?

JO. I've said I'm sorry.

BILL. It's not me you've offended.

JO. I haven't seen them to say sorry.

BILL. You know well enough where the phone is.

JO. I'll phone tomorrow.

BILL. Some of us work.

JO. I'll phone them after work and we'll just forget all about it. We've all had fights and fallen out before. But we always make up in the end though. (*To* BILL.) Don't we? (*Smelling the flowers.*) These are beginning to smell. How lovely. (*She looks out the window.*) I had a little scare this evening Bob which was perfectly natural . . .

BILL. O aye.

JO. . . . given the circumstances. It could've been avoided very
easily. (*Going to the cabinet.*) I think they're better here.
They make me so happy. Look at them! Katie's coat was
upstairs all the time. I had it in my hands. There it was. She
won't get very far without her coat and purse. She can do
whatever she wants but nobody can go anywhere without
them. You just make yourself comfortable, Bob. You can
wait here as long as you want.

BILL *hasn't looked at* JO *once during this exchange. She
looks at him, waiting for him to look up. He doesn't. She
leaves. Silence.*

BOB. I brought they flowers.

BILL. Is that right.

BOB. Aye, Katie bought some wine. I brought they flowers.

BILL. My mistake.

BOB. I was cutting the grass yesterday.

BILL. Cutting the grass?

BOB. They were left over. Fuckin' knackering it was.

BILL. I bet.

BOB. Hover mower?

BILL. This is it.

BOB. Hover mower my arse!

Pause. JO *returns with another cup.*

JO. I better set another place.

BILL. Will you leave that.

JO. What?

BILL. That.

JO. I'm just trying to salvage something from the evening.

BILL. She won't be back here the night.

JO. She has to come back.

BILL. She doesn't have to do anything.

JO. I'm sure she's not going to spend the whole evening sitting under a bus shelter. Eh, Bob?

BOB. I suppose not.

JO. No. Of course she's not. She's not at home. She couldn't have got a taxi. You're . . . well, you're here. (*Beat.*) What a funny night! (*Laughing.*) Katie's not the only thing to go missing Bill. (*Beat.*) Bill? (*Beat.*) Can you put that down for just a minute please? (*Pause.*) Bill.

BILL. What?

JO. One of my glasses has gone too. I'd nearly forgotten about it. You haven't seen it have you?

BILL. Why would I see your glass?

JO. I thought you might have. (*He continues to read.*) It's strange, that's all, that something should just vanish like that. Katie got me them Bob. She got them sent over especially. When she gave them to me the whole place came back to me instantly. A wonderful day. I could've kissed the sky. All the way from the glass island.

BOB. Murano.

JO. That's right. You remembered! I didn't show you the photo of the factory though, did I? (*Goes to brown bag.*) You'll like that. Where . . . there. (*Gives* BOB *a photo.*)

BILL. We've no time for that.

JO. Of course we have? Maybe that's where Katie wanted to go. Back there. She loved it just as much as me. (*Seeing a ticket.*) Oh! That's from the Casino. (*Reading.*) Tessera di Ingresso. That means entrance. I'd forgotten I'd even been there. That's terrible. (*Another.*) And that's from the library. (*Reading carefully.*) Biblioteca Nationale Marciana Venezia. It must be lovely to speak another language. And that's a train ticket from Venice to Trieste. James Joyce territory. He spoke dozens of languages and knew more words than Shakespeare.

BILL (*sotto voce*). Not as many as you though.

JO (*getting up and ignoring the remark*). I've got a leaflet in here I got in the train station all about him and his wife and his brother and his books. You know about him?

BILL. Will you stop harassing the lad. 'James Joyce.'

JO. Not everyone's indifferent Bill.

BILL. And clear that mess up.

JO. I thought you were reading.

BILL. I thought you were going to bed.

JO. I've still to give Bob his cheesecake.

BILL. I'm sure he's had enough excitement for one night.

JO. He's been looking forward to his cheesecake.

BOB. O aye.

JO. After what he's been through.

BOB. I like a bit of cheesecake.

Pause.

BILL'*s phone rings.*

JO. Do you ever put that thing off?

BILL (*answering the phone*). Hello. (*Aside to* BOB.) Drink up son.

BOB. Is that us?

BILL. Aye (*Getting up and talking on phone.*) Uhuh . . . Aye . . . okay . . .

JO. He's always on it.

BILL. . . . will do . . .

JO (*lightly*). Stops him having to talk to me!

BILL. . . . aye . . . okay then . . .

JO (*watching him*). But that's just him.

BILL *leaves the room to the right, still on the phone. Silence.* BOB *takes out his cigarettes. He gets up.*

BOB. I might just nip out for a quick fag.

JO. You can have a cigarette here.

BOB. I'll take it outside.

JO. Don't be silly.

BOB. I shouldn't even be here yi ken! Aye.

JO. Piece of nonsense. (*Takes shell from cabinet.*) Just use this for your ash. (*Beat.*) Where's the photo? There.

BOB. Ta.

JO (*looking in drawer*). That was a present from Viv.

BOB (*sitting down*). A present?

JO. From Florida. (*Beat.*) In America. (*Recovering photo.*) What's it doing in here? I've known her since I was five and look what she brings me back! (*Pointing to the photo.*) That's where we used to live. (*Pause.*) Me and Bill as well.

BOB. So your man was saying.

JO. Before we came up here. Five years ago. I was brought up round the corner from the flat me and Bill bought and Viv lived in the tenement two doors down. That's a summer dress I'm wearing there. I got it in Marks and Spencers on Argyle Street. Bill never liked it there. He always wanted to leave. (*Beat.*) A shell. (*Pause.*) And Mr. and Mrs. Paterson lived upstairs from us. He was blind but before that he used to take photos for the local paper. (*Beat.*) Mr. Davis lived downstairs. He was from Ireland and used to sometimes work with my Dad on the railways and his wife. (*Pause.*) She was lovely. You would've liked her. She kept an old biscuit tin under the sink in the kitchen. It must've been as old as her. It was filled with odds and ends, trinkets and bits of toys, broken scissors and a plastic duck's head I remember in particular. I used to put it over my finger like a puppet. It must have been as old as her. A duck's head.

Silence.

BOB. Ma Nan lived round there too.

JO. In Govan?

BOB. Aye.

JO. What about that!

BOB. For decades.

JO. What was her name?

BOB. Robertson.

JO. Robertson?

BOB. Aye. Like that's why I call myself Bob, not Robert, yi ken.

JO. I see, yes.

BOB. Robert Robertson. A fucking joke name that is.

JO. Robertson?

BOB. Aye.

JO. Robertson. (*Pause.*) I don't think I knew her though.

BOB. She's not there no more anyway.

JO. No?

BOB. No-one is.

JO. Oh.

BOB. They tore they old tenements down.

JO. Did they?

BOB. Aye.

JO. No.

BOB. Two year ago.

JO. They've gone too. (*Pause.*) Surely not? (*Pause.*) My childhood. (*Long pause.*) My Mum. My Dad. The washing line and the bins. (*Pause.*) All gone?

BOB. Building new flats there now.

JO. I don't know why I'm surprised to hear that. The world's always changing and . . . They were old places anyway. (*Starting to cry.*) Filthy, dirty old places. And quite ugly really. Very, very ugly, and so plain. Nothing worked either. I suppose it was inevitable that that would happen sooner or later. That they would . . . (*She takes a step to the kitchen door, nearly weeping.*) Inevitable . . . will you excuse me a . . .

BILL *returns.*

BILL. Alright then.

JO. Bill.

BILL. That's me running Bob to the station.

JO (*trying to be upbeat*). You were so right! All this time. Bob was just telling me about the old place. They've pulled it down.

BILL. Aye, a couple of years ago. I'm sure I told you.

JO (*without reproach*). You tell me nothing! Absolutely nothing. I have to get it from Bob. You were right to move here. I'm the one that's been silly. Hankering after things. (*With anger at self.*) I'm so full of such stupid, ignorant ideas. I hate them. I wish they'd leave me alone so I can get on with my life. (*Gathering the brown bag and its contents.*) I'll put all this away for a start. It's all so alien to me. This is where we live. I need to start thinking of that. (*Reading a ticket.*) Ingresso. (*She scrunches it up.*) Not this rubbish. I need to start thinking about getting back to work as well. I have to be realistic. I have to start doing things. The hospital will be opening soon. The towns will be empty, people will come up here and fill all the houses and cover the fields. Spring's coming as well. Today was sunny and bright. Everything begins again and our life here will begin as well. Tonight you even gave me a kiss hello when you came in! The first time in years. Everything does begin again. I just wish you'd told me about the old place Bill. I think that's all I needed to hear. It's like a weight lifted, a clear wind. I'll never have to think of it again. (*Putting the bag away . . .*) Or this (. . . *and the photo.*) Or . . . What a difference it's made!

BILL. I did tell you.

JO. I'm sure I would've remembered.

BILL. Let's not debate the fact.

JO. No. Let's not. No more disagreements. (*Beat.*) I'll just get us some cheesecake and we can sit down together, Katie'll be back any minute as well. It'll just be the four of us, as we intended, and the evening can end properly at least. (*Beat.*) Finally!

BILL. He's got to get the train Jo.

JO. You can't invite someone over to dinner and not give them a pudding.

BILL. We've not had dinner Jo.

JO. Stop being stupid. I know we've not had dinner.

BILL. So it doesn't make any difference whether he has a pudding or not.

JO. It does.

BOB. It's no bother.

JO. I can get you a slice as well.

BILL. Come on Bob.

JO. Please.

BILL. I'm not standing about here all night waiting for a piece of cheesecake Jo.

JO. Sit down for a moment.

BILL (*opens the door and leaves*). His train's at 11.27.

JO. He can get the next one.

BILL (*off-stage*). There's isn't a next one.

BOB. That's the last one.

JO. Is it?

BOB. Aye.

JO. No wonder he's in such a hurry to go then. (*Beat.*) He can have a slice when he gets back. You can have a slice when you come up tomorrow.

BOB. I've a job down South tomorrow.

BOB *heads for the door.*

JO. You can come in and say hello anyway.

BOB. I'll be up too early for that.

JO. We're up at the crack of dawn ourselves with the builders and the diggers.

BOB. Some noise they must make.

JO. Oh yes, dig, dig. All the time. It's so encouraging to see all the activity and progress.

The sound of a car horn is heard.

BOB (*starts to go*). That's your man there.

JO. You must let us know at least if Katie turns up at your place.

BOB. She won't turn up there.

JO. She might.

BOB (*horn again*). She doesn't know where I live.

JO. Doesn't she?

BOB. I doubt if I'll see her again.

JO. You can't think like that.

BOB. I just drove a van for her, yi ken, I didn't know her that well.

JO. Well I'm only sorry we didn't get a chance to get to know you better.

BOB. Aye.

JO. Goodbye then.

BOB. Goodbye yourself.

BOB *goes out the door.* JO *stays where she is. She then walks over to the window's and sees* KATIE*'s coat.*

JO. Katie's coat.

She picks it up. As she leans over to pick it up she notices something behind the chair. She reaches over and quickly pulls back her arm. She looks at her finger as it bleeds. She looks again behind the chair. She then lifts up a piece of broken glass. She stands up and steps away from the chair. BILL *returns.*

Oh, Bill.

BILL (*pointing to coat*). You've got it.

JO. Yes.

BILL. Bob better take it.

JO. Of course.

JO*'s finger bleeds.*

BILL. Are you alright there?

JO. I'm fine. (*Beat.*) I've just cut my finger.

BILL. As long as that's all.

JO. What else would it be? I just found my glass. That's all.
My missing Venetian glass. It was broken, there, behind the
chair. (*Beat.*) At least we know where that went.

BILL. Aye. I suppose.

JO. That's something anyway.

*Pause. They face each other for a moment, each waiting for the
other to move.*

BILL. You better see to that cut.

JO. You better not keep Robert waiting.

BILL. Bob.

JO. Bob, Robert. (*Beat.*) Whoever.

JO *looks at him straight and steady for a moment and then
exits through the kitchen door. BILL waits a moment and
looks about the room in no certain way. He goes to the
chair and picks up the coat. He looks about the room again
and then leaves with the coat. Silence. JO returns from the
kitchen with a dustpan and brush. The sound of a car
starting and then the flash of its lights followed by the
sound of it going. She stands still a moment until quiet
settles. JO then pushes the chair to the side, indifferent to
the fact that she marks the arm of the chair with the blood
from her finger. The broken glass litters the floor. JO starts
to sweep up the broken glass. Blackout.*

A Nick Hern Book

Green Field first published in Great Britain in 2002
as a paperback original by Nick Hern Books Limited,
14 Larden Road, London W3 7ST

Green Field copyright © 2002 Riccardo Galgani

Riccardo Galgani has asserted his right to be identified
as the author of this work

Typeset by Country Setting, Kingsdown, Kent CT14 8ES
Printed and bound in Great Britain by Biddles of Guildford

A CIP catalogue record for this book is available from
the British Library

ISBN 1 85459 704 3